Roger Roemmich

DON'T EAT DOG FOOD WHEN YOU'RE OLD!

Don't Eat Dog Food When You're Old!

How to Solve Your Retirement Cash Flow Puzzle

Roger Roemmich

iUniverse, Inc.
Bloomington

DON'T EAT DOG FOOD WHEN YOU'RE OLD!
HOW TO SOLVE YOUR RETIREMENT CASH FLOW PUZZLE

iUniverse books may be ordered through booksellers or by contacting:

iUniverse
1663 Liberty Drive
Bloomington, IN 47403
www.iuniverse.com
1-800-Authors (1-800-288-4677)

ISBN: 978-1-4759-8715-7 (sc)
ISBN: 978-1-4759-8716-4 (hc)
ISBN: 978-1-4759-8717-1 (e)

Library of Congress Control Number: 2013907070

Printed in the United States of America

iUniverse rev. date: 6/6/2013

Contents

About the Author

Roger Roemmich is chief investment officer of ROKA Wealth Strategists (www.rokawealthstrategists.com), a registered investment advisory firm and an IRS-approved continuing education provider with two locations in Georgia and one in Chicago. The company serves a broad base of clients, but its chief mission can be summed up in the words behind the acronym in its name: Retirement Options, Knowledgeable Advice. Roemmich advises clients on the expansive spectrum of issues related to retirement—investments, Social Security, Medicare, and long-term care, to name just a few of the big ones. He holds a PhD in accounting from Michigan State University. He is also a certified public accountant, financial planner, and long-term care professional with nearly four decades of experience in the financial arena. Roemmich is the creator of CAMP SCORE, a "retirement readiness" evaluator, which can be found at www.rrralliance.com.

Introduction

OVER THE YEARS, IT'S amazed me to observe how many of my clients simply don't look closely at the big picture of their future or current retirement plans. When it comes to their investments, they're rabidly interested in how to make their money grow. That high level of interest on the investment front is great, especially during what financial people call the accumulation stage. If you are a baby boomer, chances are you're working hard to pay your mortgage, your homeowner's insurance, your car insurance, your car payment(s), your household bills, your medical bills, and possibly college tuition for one or more of your kids. Chances are you're trying to build up your 401(k) as well (I hope you are!). You're squarely in the accumulation stage, even though the outflow of cash to sustain your basic standard of living, whatever that may be, might seem so huge that saving for your eventual retirement strikes you as nearly impossible. Even so, if you're a sensible person, I'm sure you've got your eye on the retirement ball, at least to some extent.

If you are close to retirement age, which is currently sixty-six from a Social Security standpoint, you're probably still focused on your investments, which isn't necessarily the best thing for you to be doing, at least not entirely. In view of the recent recession, you may be wondering where your investments went. They may have flown the proverbial coop and are only now just recovering. If you're like most people in your position, you're probably thinking about how to make your money back as fast as possible so that you can tell the boss to stick it and head out for endless rounds of golf or games of mah-jongg. Again, that's not bad on the face of it. In fact, it's perfectly natural, but it shouldn't be the only issue on your mind. If it is, you're missing the big picture about your retirement planning.

If you are currently retired, you're probably fixated on your investments as well. You're probably hugely annoyed over the historically low interest rates that have killed your returns on certificates of deposit and relatively safe money market funds, forcing you to take risks in the stock market with what investments you have left after the financial meltdown in recent years. You're probably very worried about what's going to happen to you down the road from a financial perspective. You could be a person of robust means, but still you worry! You may not be seeing the big picture about how to bail yourself out of a potentially worrisome retirement either.

Some Cautionary Tales

Tale 1: During the early 1990s I advised a couple in their fifties. They had been married about five years (it was the second marriage for both). They had about $150,000 in housing equity and about $80,000 in IRAs. They were determined to retire and move from their metropolitan home to the mountains of North Carolina. I advised them that they didn't have nearly enough assets to retire, because neither of them would even be eligible for Social Security for eight more years. They both said, "We want out of the rat race we work in every day. If we run short of money, we will simply sell real estate part-time!" They ignored my advice and headed to the hills.

Three years later, I asked their CPA how they were doing. He said they had divorced and both had gone back to work in real estate.

Tale 2: A longtime client had a very responsible job, but she hated it. She felt she couldn't take it any longer. My partner and I literally begged her not to do anything rash. However, when she reached sixty-two, she retired and began drawing Social Security. Unfortunately, her husband lost his job at about the same time, and he also began drawing his Social Security at age sixty-two. Both of them looked for work, but after a year and a half, neither one had found work they liked. Their investment assets of $200,000 left them with inadequate cash flow to weather the financial storm, a storm they partially brought on themselves.

So retiring prematurely and a job loss forced my clients to take Social Security early. As a result, both got hit with a 25 percent penalty on their benefits, versus if they had waited to draw their full benefits at age sixty-six. Drawing Social Security early is a very common mistake, even without a job loss factored into the retirement equation.

My business partner and I advised our client and her husband to do something that struck them both as totally radical. We suggested that they draw from their $200,000 in IRAs to pay back their Social Security benefits. They thought we were crazy. Indeed, neither of them knew they actually could pay back Social Security benefits under certain conditions, and cashing in some of their IRA to do it didn't make sense. However, after we did the math for them regarding the value in Social Security benefits that they'd given up, they saw the wisdom of our advice. They are drawing $3,000 a month from their IRAs while they look for work. The good news is, they haven't plundered their very valuable Social Security benefits.

Tale 3: We have had several clients cash out their IRAs/ retirement plan balances to make a down payment on a second home in a resort area. By doing so, they

- paid a large amount of taxes up-front to liquidate their IRAs,
- decreased their base for future cash flows, and
- increased their monthly cash flow needs to make payments on the resort home.

We begged these clients to think things through before making such potentially ruinous decisions. Sometimes, it's sad to say, you can lead a horse to water but you can't make it drink.

The point of these tales is that even very bright and successful people do stupid things, especially when it comes to retirement. They don't look at the big picture. They fixate on accumulating assets, retaining assets, scrimping on Medicare plans, or raiding their hard-earned Social Security benefits early. Investments form just a piece of your retirement puzzle. They're very, very important, but there are other pieces of the puzzle to contend with as well—proper management of your Social Security (and the Social Security of your spouse), Medicare, long-term care (LTC), asset drawdown sequences, risk assessment, inflation protection, and cash flow.

The latter area, cash flow, is the very foundation of your retirement and the key premise of this book. Cash flow is king in retirement. Intuitively, you may think cash flow is tied directly to your investments, which is why you worry about them so much, especially in these tough economic times. And you'd be absolutely right. Investments do provide cash flow, but some do it better than others. For example, sometimes it's better to buy an alternate investment, such as a piece of a real estate investment trust (REIT) that is not liquid, than it is to buy a growth stock that is liquid. And don't forget about Social Security. It may represent the biggest source of cash flow you have, and yet you might consider taking it early. You may also resist with all your intellectual strength any suggestion to defer taking it until you hit age seventy. I bet you would on both counts.

I'll get into all of this in detail in the coming pages. You'll get a big-picture look at what you need to know to plan for your retirement or to better manage the various components of your financial life if you already are retired. The package is a puzzle, but you can figure out how to fit all the pieces together with the help you'll receive in this book.

One more thing: It's important to take responsibility for your own money. Learn and keep learning. Educate yourself about Social Security, Medicare, and long-term care. This book is a great start, but it shouldn't be the only source you use. I highly recommend the website of the American Association of Retired People, commonly known as AARP (www.aarp.org). There's tons of sound data and advice on the site that you can use as you poke around, looking for any information you may not have found here. The Social Security website is another terrific source (www.ssa.gov). Those are just two places to look. The information you need is available to you. You just have to want to find it. You have to want to use it too.

So let's begin! You're in for an intriguing ride, I can tell you that. There is information in this book about a wide variety of subjects related to retirement you won't find anywhere else.

On with the journey!

I

Retirement Landmines 101

So you're thinking of retiring, or you're already there. It's an exciting time, and you're certainly not alone in turning the page on a brand-new chapter in your life. An estimated seventy-eight million baby boomers will hit retirement age in the coming decades, with 2011 marking the first wave of boomers hitting the golden shores of so-called retirement paradise. Just so you know, the US Census Bureau classifies you as a baby boomer if you were born between 1946 and 1964. It's always struck me as a rather arbitrary label. After all, boomers were supposed to have resulted from the influx of millions of American servicemen flocking home to raise families at the end of World War II. I'd have thought they'd have been pretty tired after eighteen years of baby booming into the mid-1960s, but I guess not. At any rate, boomers are reshaping the nature of life in the United States as they grow older and retire, so you've got plenty of company if you're part of the gang.

According to a 2012 report from AARP, a staggering eight thousand boomers will turn sixty-five every day for the next eighteen years. That's a lot of people looking at retirement and considering whether they should quit their day job to go do something fun. I'll get into more detail on deciding whether you can afford to retire in the next chapter, and in later chapters I'll get into specific areas that represent the core of sound strategic retirement planning and financial management once you do retire. But let's first take a quick look at some statistics that will shed some light on the current realities many of you may be facing.

Consider that most boomers in decent health will live well into their nineties. Good enough! Living into your nineties means you had a pretty fine run. Now consider how much money you'll need from investments, Social Security, a pension (if you're one of the lucky few who have one), and other sources of income. Feeling depressed yet? If you think you need a boatload of cash, you're right, in some respects, and if you don't have significant assets, there is some cause for concern. But the boatload of cash isn't your sole ticket to the Emerald City. It only represents part of the package.

Were you taught that asset accumulation was the Holy Grail of retirement preparation? Chances are you were, but that kind of thinking is outdated and even a bit dangerous nowadays. With two meltdowns in the stock market just over a decade apart, the resounding burst of the real estate bubble, interest rates at historic lows, and the added emotional and financial responsibilities of what has been called the sandwich generation—folks like you who have to take care of kids under the age of twenty-one and elderly parents to boot—you've got a pretty daunting reality to face when you think about retiring.

A Harris Interactive poll taken in 2011, the year, as you recall, that the first wave of boomers hit the retirement beach, reveals some astonishing realities. The poll surveyed adults ages forty-six to sixty-four and seniors age sixty-five and up. Twenty-six percent of the respondents age forty-six to sixty-four reported having no personal savings at all, and 25 percent of this group reported having no retirement savings at all. The statistics were pretty dismal for the age sixty-five and up crowd too. Fourteen percent reported having no personal savings at all, and 25 percent reported having no retirement savings at all.

That's pretty scary. It means retirement is a pipe dream for many people, millions in fact. However, if you look at those numbers from the other side, it means that the majority of people do have some financial assets to work with during their retirement. The dollar value of those assets may not be very encouraging for some of you, but if you have something to work with, then there's hope. You can look down the road and envision a brighter future. Really, you can! It just takes some innovative thinking, and one of the most important shifts in thought is to get away from the sole focus on accumulating financial assets (though that's vital, of course) and focus on how to maximize your cash flow during retirement. As I said in the introduction, that's what this book is all about.

The first step in moving forward with an active retirement plan, or with measures to tweak your current retirement management strategy, if you've already taken the plunge, is to look at the most common mistakes people make when it comes to retirement. Some of them might sound pretty obvious. You may say, "Oh, heck no! I'd never do that!" But if you peel back the layers of the onion, you might be surprised to see that you've stepped on one or more of the retirement landmines listed below. Take a look; you might get a wakeup call.

I'll get into much more detail on all the subjects below as we take our journey together through the twists and turns of sound financial planning and management that will help make sure you have the cash flow you need in your golden years. Knowing where the landmines are before we start out is a great way to get set to go.

Top twelve retirement landmines

Retirement Landmine 1: Retiring too early

Let's face it. Most of us would love to retire. If you're like most people in the labor force, you've got a job, but you're not doing work you love. You're doing a job to get money to support yourself and your family, and that's it. So it's no surprise that when you hit retirement age, you want to run screaming for the door. The problem is you may shoot yourself in the foot financially if you do. Income from a job is your greatest source of cash flow. Think twice before you ditch it. Hang in there for as long as you can. Also, bear in mind that your final decade of work is likely to be your highest-paid period.

Retirement Landmine 2: Failing to go back to work when you realize you retired too early

This is a big deal. If you're struggling to make ends meet because you lack sufficient cash flow after you retire, the fastest way to improve the quality of your life is to go back to work. It doesn't have to be a forty-hour slog. A part-time job can really help. The problem is many people feel like failures if they have to go back to work. There's a real psychological whammy to get over. Another major hurdle is the kind of jobs you are likely to get. Some people look down their noses and make jokes about the blue-hair greeters in Walmart, but the folks you see at the door are getting a paycheck. The same goes for the older ladies and gents you see in the deli department at the supermarket, working right beside the college kids. No job is too lowly if you need the money. If you take active steps to improve your cash flow when you realize you've fallen short, then you're the winner. You are anything but a loser or a failure.

Retirement Landmine 2 plays right into the next issue. If you run screaming from the room in the job you have before you retire, you might have to settle for a lesser paying and possibly less fulfilling job if you are forced to reenter the labor force. That's why it's so important to view taking the retirement plunge as one of the most important life decisions you'll ever make. Don't shoot first and ask questions later. Go into the decision with as much information as you can get.

Retirement Landmine 3: Failing to invest retirement assets to produce cash flow

This might sound really strange at first. Who wouldn't invest their money to produce cash flow? You'd actually be surprised at how many retirees drop the ball in this department, especially those in the first wave of the baby boomers and even more so with preboomers. Too many of us focus on stocks or mutual funds, which are volatile and risky. Bonds are safer and produce predictable returns, but there are risks involved with them too. The point is you have more options than the tried and true investment vehicles, such as an annuity, to produce cash flow and minimize risk.

If you take only one point home from Retirement Landmine 3, it should be this: Don't leave excessive amounts of cash sitting in savings accounts or money market funds, which haven't paid a decent return since 2007. If interest rates rise dramatically in the future, then having some of your assets tied up in savings accounts, certificates of deposit, and money market funds might make more sense, as long as you take a balanced approach. Right now, though, excessive cash in these vehicles makes little or no sense and robs you of opportunities to take advantage of the money you've got to build for your retirement (or live a better quality of life if you're already retired).

Got burned in the stock market? Twice? Join the club. Don't let your nightmare lead you to such a level of risk aversion that you sit on your cash. There are plenty of less risky things you can do with your cash so that it will work harder for you than taking a stuff-the-bucks-in-the-mattress approach because you got clobbered in two stock market disasters.

Retirement Landmine 4: Beginning Social Security benefits too soon

This is a huge mistake that more and more people of retirement age make. The reasons are easy to figure out. Lots of us got burned in two meltdowns in the stock market. The value of our real estate tanked during the recession. Interest rates are practically zero, which means traditional methods of saving don't work anymore. It all seems pretty hopeless, doesn't it? So it's natural to grab the bird in the hand instead of leaving it chirping happily away in the bush. The problem is, if you take Social Security too soon, you rob yourself of an opportunity for greater cash flow down the road. You also rob your spouse if you die first. He or she will get a heftier survivor's benefit if you wait until full retirement age (FRA) before taking Social Security. Better still, why not defer taking Social Security until you hit age seventy? You can earn an 8 percent annualized return between the age of sixty-six and seventy. By doing so four years of an extra 8 percent per year adds 32 percent per year to your benefits at age seventy. Don't monthly Social Security benefits of 132 percent of what you would have received starting benefits at age sixty-six sound good? They can be yours!

Drawing Social Security at age sixty-two causes retirees born between 1943 and 1954 to lose 25 percent per year of their potential Social Security benefits for life, versus waiting until full retirement age of sixty-six. If you can wait to collect 100 percent of your Social Security benefits, you should do so. The loss of 25 percent of your benefits adds up fast. Besides, where else are you going to get that kind of return on your money risk free?

Retirement Landmine 5: Choosing a Medicare plan based on price rather than picking an option that really protects you

You might think you're doing yourself a favor by picking the cheapest possible coverage. You say, "Hey, I'm improving cash flow since I'm having to pay less every month." Sounds great in theory, right? Wrong! Medicare doesn't pay for everything, and in some cases, if you face a serious illness or injury, with the wrong options you could go broke in a hurry. There's a saying you've no doubt heard, possibly as a kid: penny wise and pound foolish. Don't skimp on health care. It could come back to bite you.

**Retirement Landmine 6: Not having a
reasonable long-term care plan**

This one is a real bogeyman for many people. First, it's really depressing to think you might need long-term care (LTC) because of a stroke, serious injury, or dementia of some sort. It's natural to want to bury your head in the sand and forget about it. The other objection is money. Long-term care insurance costs big bucks. Even economical plans can cost around $3,000 per year for a person who's sixty-five, which is why most sources say fewer than 10 percent of all seniors actually have coverage.

The reality is between 2000 and 2040, the number of seniors with disabilities, many of which make them candidates for long-term care, is projected to double, impacting about twenty-one million of us, according to the American Association of Long-Term Care Insurance (AALTCI). That's almost 25 percent of the nearly eighty million boomers. Put another way, one out of four of us will likely require some form of long-term care during our retirement years. Other sources say the figure is closer to 75 percent. Even splitting the difference should be enough to keep you up at night, if you're unprotected.

Losing your entire life's savings, or that of your spouse, is a very distinct possibility if you require extensive and prolonged long-term care. Annual median costs generally exceed $73,000, and increase if you need a lot of services. For example, recent data from the US Department of Health and Human Services indicates that the average daily cost of a semiprivate room in a nursing home is $198, or a whopping $72,270 per year. Unless you are really wealthy, it's highly unlikely that you can afford to self-insure against the risk of serious illness or dementia that requires prolonged long-term care.

Not having long-term care insurance is laying the groundwork for financial disaster for you or your spouse, and it's as risky as not having any health care insurance at all, something you'd be unlikely to accept if you could afford even basic health care coverage. I find it both surprising and misinformed when I read that single persons need LTC insurance or alternative protection more than married couples. If a single person suffers a long-term infirmity, they will be forced to rely on Medicaid, unless they have very substantial means. Single persons need LTC, but married couples risk not only their own financial resources but also their spouse's resources. The financial strain on the spouse adds to the emotional and physical strain of dealing with an infirmed spouse.

Consider the effect when a married person suffers a long-term infirmity. Medicaid will provide for their care but take their monthly income and nearly all their assets. Unfortunately, Medicaid permits spouses to have only a monthly maintenance amount and a minimal amount of assets (less than $100,000) that are not devoted to paying for the infirmed spouse's care. Thus, LTC affects not only the infirmed but also their spouse, who often suffers physiologically, psychologically, and financially. Have an LTC plan to protect the spouse you love and cherish.

Many of you are probably despairing a bit. You know you need long-term care coverage, but you think you just can't afford it. I'll discuss options for you to consider in chapter 11.

Retirement Landmine 7: Failing to recognize the need for increasing cash flow to match inflation in future years

It's not enough to set up your retirement to ensure you have adequate cash flow, though that's a heck of a great start. As you plan and select instruments to deploy, bear the inflation monsters in mind. It's lurking around the bend. Build in cost-of-living increases into the equation whenever possible.

Retirement Landmine 8: Placing too much emphasis on providing a financial legacy for heirs, thereby risking your own financial stability

I once knew an elderly lady who had lived frugally all her life. When Tina hit age eighty-two, she went out and bought a brand-new Mercedes.

Those cars start at around fifty grand. I said, "Nice car, Tina! What made you go for it?"

She laughed and said, "I didn't save all my life just to leave my money to my kids!"

An increasing number of boomers are seeing things the way Tina does, especially those of us who got "sandwiched" along the way. And yet, some cling to the "legacy" way of thinking, and they pay the price in lower quality of life, increased anxiety, stress that creates physical problems, and so on. Look out for yourself and your spouse first. The kids can generally take care of themselves.

Retirement Landmine 9: Retiring with too much debt

You'd be amazed at how many people punch out for the last time at work and waltz home with credit card debts, boat payments, two car payments, time-share obligations, and a hefty mortgage. If you're really loaded and have plenty of guaranteed cash flow, I suppose it's okay to do this, but even then I still wouldn't encourage it. If you're already playing close to the edge of financial cash flow comfort, then I'd say you might do well to rethink whether you should retire at all. Payment of debt obligations should be minimized or even eliminated *before* you retire, not after.

Retirement Landmine 10: Drawing retirement cash flow from volatile investments, causing liquidation while investments are depressed

The old way of thinking is you accumulate lots of money, diversify your stock portfolio, and then draw on the returns in dividends and share value increases to fund your monthly cash flow needs. If you tried this in the last twelve years or so, you got kicked in the teeth. You've had to sell when the market was in the tank, not only losing principal but also facing negative returns on the existing investments.

Thinking outside the box would help reduce your liability. For example, if you had purchased a whole-life insurance policy in the late 1990s from a reputable insurance company, your investment would have been protected from loss. That's just one example of creative thinking you can apply to your retirement planning and management.

Retirement Landmine 11: Failing to keep up with changes in society and in the markets

It pays to follow your investments with care. Stocks in a given sector definitely go out of favor. Sectors represented in mutual funds do too. Keeping your finger on the pulse of current trends will help you respond to inevitable changes. Meeting with your financial professionals and asking intelligent questions based on the knowledge you have accumulated will help as well. Lastly, investment vehicles like annuities can come back in favor, as they are now, whereas they were looked down on a decade or so ago. Reverse mortgages were once considered only for suckers, but now with the right plan they can become part of your overall cash flow strategy, though I'm still not crazy about them; call me Mr. Conservative! The point is that things change. You need to be aware of those changes, and you need to be proactive, not reactive.

Retirement Landmine 12: Not finding or seeking qualified advice

Even millionaires and very savvy investors have advisers. If you're in this elite club, you know you need qualified professional help to manage your wealth. If you're laughing ruefully and saying you don't have any wealth to manage, chances are you're wrong. If you have some money put by in some financial vehicle, you've got wealth. It may not be the "book a room at the Plaza" kind, but you still need qualified financial advisers, and possibly an accountant and tax adviser. Only you can determine the level of expertise you need. Choose your advisers wisely. The advice they give and that you follow can determine how you live out the rest of your life.

2

Can You Afford to Retire?

WITH MORE THAN EIGHT thousand baby boomers hitting the magic age of sixty-five every day in the United States, and with millions more of us waiting in the wings, questions about retiring are bound to come up pretty much anywhere and at any time. At the top of the list for many of us is whether retirement is even possible. Let's face it: the world is a much different place than it was for our parents and grandparents. The global economy has transformed life in America, and not always for the best. The stark realities of a harsh economic environment are hitting boomers now more than ever before, and don't expect things to change. If anything, the going will get tougher, not easier.

That said, there's no reason to despair. If you know you've got a steep mountain to climb, you buy the right hiking boots and just get going. We have to make realistic decisions about what we're supposed to do to prepare for those so-called golden years armed with the knowledge we need to put ourselves in a good place from a financial, physical, emotional, psychological, and social perspective. There's no doubt that you've asked yourself if you can afford to retire. If you've already retired, it's safe to say you've asked yourself whether you can stay retired or if you have enough money to live until you're in your midnineties without running out of cash. There are no easy answers. But I'm here to say you've probably got more arrows in your quiver than you might think.

Timing is everything

Financial security and the quality of your retirement experience require you to time your retirement properly. Very few retirees express regret that they retired too late. Many successful people regret retiring too early. The incremental effect of working one or two more years beyond age sixty-five can dramatically improve retirement cash flows, so don't be in too much of a rush to collect your Social Security benefits and pocket the gold watch at your retirement dinner.

Retiring too early presents major risks to the quality of your life after you punch out permanently from work. Most of us earn our highest compensation just prior to retirement. We're putting in the most cash to fund our future Social Security benefits, and we're using our highest earnings to fund our asset pool, the one that we'll need to organize properly to maintain the cash flow we'll need when we finally do call it quits. If you retire too early, you most likely will find it hard, if not impossible, to reproduce your current income streams if you discover too late that you retired too soon and lack the cash flow necessary to meet expenses.

It may sound obvious, but I must say it anyway: savings result when income exceeds cash flow needs. When you retire, it's quite likely that you won't be able to save much, if anything. You'll be relying on returns from investments and additional cash flow from a corporate or government pension and Social Security. So look at work as a way to build for the future through savings, a way to defer taking Social Security, and a way to put off drawing down your assets.

Pointer: Don't retire too early, even if you hate your job. Once you leave, you probably can't come back.

The three-legged stool needs crutches

We've all heard it before, the guff about the three-legged stool. You know what I'm talking about. In the good old days, we were told we could rely on a government or corporate pension, Social Security, and personal investments to get us through our old age. If we were lucky, we'd even have enough money to go to Boca with our sweetheart or to Disney World with the grandkids. Those three financial components were called the three-legged stool.

Nowadays, lots of seniors or soon-to-be retirees only have one and a half legs on their stool; the only leg left intact is Social Security. The half leg is what's left of their investments after two major financial disasters in just over a decade. The new millennium hasn't been kind to us boomers, especially the younger ones. According to the most recently available data from the US Bureau of Labor, the percentage of workers participating in defined benefit pension plans fell from 38 percent to 20 percent between 1980 and 2008. That means 80 percent of us are missing a leg from our stool, and we're wondering just how we're supposed to sit comfortably with that absence.

I generally modify the components of the three-legged stool to include retirement income from part-time work. Yes, I know, you retired to play golf, spoil the grandkids, and hit the road in the Winnebago, but you probably won't be a full-time retiree. That's the cold, hard truth for most of us. For those of you who are lucky enough to have a fully functioning stool, you've still got an incentive to pursue part-time work to enhance your cash flow opportunities. And if you haven't retired yet, I hope you think twice before you do so until you're certain the time is right. Retirement isn't something to jump into lightly.

The poor investment environment since 2000 has depleted the projected reserves of many baby boomers. Part-time employment may allow you to retire with fewer assets. Part-time income can either reduce your monthly shortfall or allow you to continue accumulating assets. During the time period between 1980 and 2000, most financial planners generally assumed a 5 or 6 percent investment cash flow from investments. Reduced income opportunities since 2000 have lowered cash flow potential. Financial advisers and investment management firms now advise projecting only 4 percent or even 3.5 percent cash flow from investments—if you're lucky.

Declining income streams from safe and easy-to-understand investments, like certificates of deposit (CDs: remember those?), have combined with increasing medical and living expenses, and longer life expectancies, to threaten your retirement quality of life. Increased life expectancy during retirement expands the need to make investments that continue to provide cash flow for an extended period. It is critical to understand the difference between principal and income, and I'm sorry to say that each year, fewer seniors behave like they have this understanding. Consuming principal reduces future cash flow/income for retirees. Thus, every investment should be evaluated based on current and future cash flow/income. Some investments have a limited term (life), and others have declining income. I'll go into much more detail later, but the bottom line is, when you retire, you'd best not deplete principal, because once it's gone, it ain't coming back.

As a child I read a fable about the Golden Goose. The Golden Goose laid a gold egg every day. Unfortunately, the goose's owner became greedy and cut open the Golden Goose to get what was inside. Now the owner no longer had the goose and didn't get a new shiny gold egg every day. Consuming principal kills the Golden Goose that produces future income. How wise our elders were, and how wise we are if we remember the lessons they tried to teach us! Don't kill the Golden Goose; preserve your principal.

Pointer: Working part-time after you retire can allow you to retire with fewer overall assets, and it can protect the principal you have by creating additional cash flow.

Look at it this way: Marginal income is the last income earned. If you earn $1,000 per month and get a 10 percent raise, you have $100 of marginal income. If you do not raise your spending level, that $100 becomes savings. Thus, marginal income from a second job or working during retirement can have a powerful effect on your quality of life.

Assets are great, but cash flow is king

Focusing on asset accumulation during the preretirement years helps retirees get where they need to be prior to retirement. But the single biggest retirement planning mistake people make is emphasizing asset accumulation rather than net cash flows. Focusing on asset accumulation and asset retention frequently causes retirees to make terrible retirement decisions. Two potentially disastrous decisions retirees make when trying to grow or maintain assets are poorly timing the beginning of their Social Security benefits and failing to purchase Medicare supplements and long-term care (LTC) protection.

Pointer: Projected retirement cash flows must match or exceed retirement cash expenditures. Cash flow, *not* assets, should be viewed as the central premise (variable) for planning retirement. Sufficient cash flow allows retirees to do the following:

- meet physiological (food, shelter, and health care) needs
- buy Medicare Part D drug coverage and Medicare supplement insurance *or* elect an appropriate Medicare Advantage plan
- interact socially with friends and family

Cash flows may be positive or negative. Obviously, you want positive cash flow when you retire, so don't focus too much on the asset side of the retirement equation without seriously looking at the cash flow side. For example, what good is it to own $2 million in land that produces no income and leaves you with two bucks in the bank? On paper, you'd be a millionaire, but you'd also be cash flow poor.

Consider all of the following as cash flow sources and therefore part of the retirement allocation process:

- investments
- Social Security
- corporate or government pension

- full- or part-time work
- equity credit in your home

"Now just hold on for a minute," you're saying. "Cash flow from equity credit? What's up with that?"

Surprisingly enough, equity credit can factor into your retirement strategy if you've got good reasons to go that route, and if it makes sense for you. Like I said, don't sweat the assets at the cost of neglecting your retirement cash flow. Figuring out the cash flow aspect of your retirement in advance of taking the plunge will tell you better than anything else whether you can actually afford to retire. Looking to home equity credit made pretty good sense for some of us in 2012.

Here's why:

- Interest rates on equity loans are at sixty-year lows.
- Social Security increases for deferring retirement benefits have increased to 8 percent per year between full retirement age (FRA) and age seventy.
- Variable annuities with living benefits and pensions generally guarantee increased cash flow payments if benefits are deferred.
- Reinvestment rates in nontraded public REITs typically exceed interest rates on equity loans.

Note that Social Security, variable annuities with living benefits, and nontraded public REITs all generate cash flow growth that significantly exceeds the cost of equity loans on home equity. Seniors, loved ones, advisers, and government/industry regulators often place too much emphasis upon liquidity and not enough on cash flow considerations.

Protecting against adverse cash flow expenses may be more important than producing cash flow income. Medicare and long-term care protection (not necessarily insurance) should be considered *essential* to a good retirement plan. Failure to protect against these risks endangers quality of life for retirees and those close to them.

Building a margin of safety into retirement projections will hopefully enable you to enjoy retirement because your physiological needs are met *and* you feel able to pursue growth needs because your cash flow needs have been met. Developing new interests (or pursuing old interests) should be one of the joys of retirement. You need cash flow to do it.

Inflation can easily erode a retiree's quality of life. Investments and distribution choices should build in either purchasing power increases or a margin of safety sufficient to meet inflationary pressures. Future cash flow increases must *outpace* future cash flow needs.

Cash flow versus expenses

Project retirement expenses to match your monthly income just prior to retirement to make sure a margin of safety exists. Planning retirement income is much easier than planning retirement expenses. Thus, make current income the *base* starting point in retirement planning. Potential retirees who focus on reproducing their net working income, as opposed to meeting projected expenses, are far more likely to succeed in achieving a satisfying and fulfilling life during retirement. In planning, utilize a projected 4 or 5 percent increase in retirement cash flow. This allows for the probability of any unexpected adverse event.

A very common retirement planning mistake occurs when individuals or couples project receiving income from all of their assets and also assumes those same assets are available to meet needs for emergency funds, long-term care needs, an inheritance for their spouse/children, household projects, and other personal desires. Seldom will retirement expenses match current living expenses (they are usually lower), but using current after-tax income as the planning starting point solves the following difficulties:

- Few people can (or will) accurately assess current and future expenses.
- Unforeseen retirement expenses derail the quality of retirement life for a large percentage of retirees.
- People often retire too early because key variables were underestimated or forgotten. This creates stress because it is very difficult to return to working at the same income level.
- Most people do not want to risk the chance that their unexpected financial needs will become a burden to their spouse or loved ones. Providing for or covering *sustaining* factors will lessen or eliminate risks of unexpected financial needs.

Retirement should begin only after most retirement variables have been explored and any medical or cash flow exposures have been addressed. Quitting your job should *only* occur once steps have been taken to ensure an appropriate margin of safety. Projected monthly retirement cash inflows should exceed retirement cash expenses, unless you are willing and able to consume capital (principal).

In planning, utilize a projected 4 or 5 percent increase in retirement cash flow. This allows for the probability of any unexpected adverse event. Note the difference between cash flow generated at 4, 5, and 6 percent return on the assets.

	4%	5%	6%
$234,000	**$9,360**	**$11,700**	**$14,040**

Each 1 percent of additional investment return generates $2,340 more cash flow per year, or $195 per month. To prevent eroding assets during retirement, you may have to work part-time to make up the difference. Part-time employment during retirement should be a strong consideration to allow you to maintain cash flow and grow your assets.

What Is your CAMP Score?

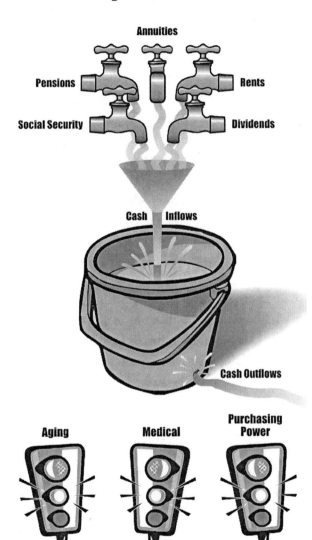

Measuring your retirement readiness

Retirement readiness is very difficult to measure, both at retirement and during the course of a long retirement. Developing a "CAMP" score will help you measure your retirement readiness. A CAMP score is a function of four key retirement concerns:

C for Cash flow. Retirement cash flow is measured as a percentage of preretirement cash flow. If you need cash flow of $5,000 per month to meet expenses while you are working, and you project your retirement cash flow at $4,500, then you are only 90 percent covered. You need to match your working cash flow (what you're bringing in now to meet expenses while you're working) to get a CAMP score of 100. If you don't score 100, then you can't afford to retire with enough of a safety margin to head trouble off at the pass. As noted, working part-time can allow you to make up the difference.

There are three other factors in determining your CAMP score. These are all likely to create declines in your cash flow or your assets. They must be taken into consideration when deciding whether you can afford to retire or not. Failure to account for them builds risk into your retirement years that could prove financially damaging and could impinge upon the quality of your life.

These sustaining factors:

A for Aging protection against potentially ruinous long-term care needs.

M for Medical and health care costs.

P for Purchasing power, which declines due to inflation. Inflation or purchasing power erosion causes cash flow to be inadequate to meet cash expenses or results in using assets to pay expenses.

A minimally prepared retiree (with no margin of safety) has a CAMP score of approximately 100. Very few retirees will have enough retirement cash flow to self-insure the sustaining factor risks. Thus, measures should be taken to protect against these risks.

Your retirement concerns likely include the following:

- medical protection
- long-term care coverage
- monthly income
- reserves for emergencies

Aging: Even if initial retirement cash flow is good, the three key sustaining factors must be addressed, or retirement quality of life is at risk. For example, most people have a longer retirement horizon due to health care advances, so the odds of large long-term care expenses rise significantly. This longevity allows for a long, wonderful retirement but also dramatically increases risks related to long-term care needs.

Medical: The second sustaining factor is medical and health care costs. Most people have reasonable corporate or business health insurance while working, but they make the mistake of trying to save a few dollars each month on Medicare costs. Unfortunately, this leads to both higher costs and way more risk or exposure to medical costs. While there are regional differences for medical costs, Medicare with Part D (drug) coverage, and Medicare Supplement Type F coverage, including Medicare Part B, the best possible coverage will typically cost between $300 and $400 per month.

Purchasing power: The third sustaining factor is purchasing power growth with inflationary cost increases. Most corporate pensions do not include an inflationary pension increase. Thus, $3,000 per month at age sixty-six may look great, but at age eighty-six, this same $3,000 per month doesn't look as good. The maximum Social Security benefit in 1990 was approximately $975 per month. Twenty-two years later, the same person with cost-of-living increases would receive just under

$1,800. The average inflationary increase is about 3 percent per year over that period. Thus, to equal $3,000 in 1990, it would take between $5,500 and $6,000 in 2012. This illustrates the importance of the purchasing power concept in the CAMP score.

When we give clients a CAMP score to judge their retirement readiness, even if their current score equals 100 (the minimum initial score to be retirement ready), lack of attention to the three sustaining factors remains likely to reduce retirement readiness. Unfortunately, the longer you have been retired, the less likely you are able to return to at least part-time work to make up the shortfall.

The Social Security factor

As I've been saying, retirement security results from having sufficient cash flow to meet monthly obligations and desires. Traditional retirement advice focuses primarily on acquiring enough assets to live securely in retirement. Cash flow from Social Security, corporate pensions, and part-time work is not ignored, but most analysis concentrates on accumulating enough assets to live comfortably. Two major investment houses recently advertised their ability to tell seniors how large an investment pool is necessary to be able to safely retire.

I find any approach based primarily on asset accumulation to be seriously flawed because of the problems of mixing cash flows and assets (versus the cash flow that assets may produce and because returns on assets have varied so dramatically over time). The table describing "How Valuable is Social Security" demonstrates how flawed that asset-based approach is. The maximum Social Security benefit in 1990 was approximately $975 for a worker reaching age sixty-five. The earning rate on a six-month certificate of deposit was 7.5 percent, and a ten-year US Treasury Bond yielded 7.94 percent. Thus, if you retired in 1990 with maximum Social Security and $100,000 invested in a six-month CD and another $100,000 invested in ten-year US Treasury Bonds, you would have initially had an annual cash flow of $27,140. The calculations are:

Social Security	$975 times 12	$11,700 (43.11%)
CD	$100,000 times 7.5%	$7,500 (27.63%)
Ten-Year Treasury	$100,000 times 7.94%	$7,940 (29.26%)
		$27,140 (100.0%)

Assuming you spent each year's Social Security and investment income, your cash flow in 2013 would be as follows:

Social Security	$1,800 times 12	$21,600 (89.26%)
CD	$100,000 times 0.63%	$630 (2.60%)
Ten-Year Treasury	$100,000 times 7.94%	$1,970 (8.14%)
		$24,200 (100.0%)

The growth in your Social Security check has not kept up with inflation, but diminished investment returns have forced you to rely more every year on your Social Security check. Social Security represented 43.11 percent of your cash flow in 1990 but would represent 89.26 percent of your cash flow in 2013. These numbers should startle you. They dramatically show how what you thought was once a good and relatively risk-free retirement plan can get turned upside down over time.

I am very concerned about a statistic that neither Congress nor the executive branch of our government seems to realize: estimates show almost one-third of Americans over age sixty-five do not get enough to eat each day. Low interest rates may work for a government burdened by too much debt and younger Americans trying to get started, but they are seriously threatening the quality of life for seniors.

How Valuable Is Social Security?				
	1990	**2000**	**2010**	**2013**
Maximum Social Security (Age 65)	$975	$1,435	$2,191	$2,365
Receiving 2013	$1,792	$1,986	$2,309	$2,365
Six-month CD	7.50%	6.75%	0.75%	0.63%
Assets required to match Social Security	$156,000	$255,111	$3,505,600	$4,504,762
Ten-Year US Treasury Bond	7.94%	6.58%	3.85%	1.97%
Assets required to match Social Security	$147,355	$261,702	$682,909	$1,440,609
Return on S&P 500 Index for last ten years	Approx. 8%	Approx. 18%	Approx. 1%	

Key conclusions:

1. It takes over thirty times the assets invested in CDs in 2013 (versus 1990) to produce less than three times the monthly Social Security income (versus 1990).

2. It take over ten times the assets invested in Ten-Year US Treasury Bonds in 2013 (versus 1990) to produce less than three times the monthly Social Security income (versus 1990).

3. The S&P 500 Index return varies wildly between decades.

4. A worker who retired at age sixty-five in 1990 with maximum benefits would receive just less than $1,800 in benefits in 2013. The increases have occurred due to Social Security cost-of-living indexes (COLAs).

Obviously, an asset-based retirement planning system is seriously flawed. It depends way too much on future investment returns. If investment returns available on assets decline, retirees will experience serious declines in retirement cash flows and quality of life. For this reason, I believe cash flow, *not* assets, is the proper basis for determining retirement readiness. The CAMP score is designed to measure the ability of a retiree to maintain net monthly cash flows during retirement and meet the inevitable increases in medical costs, long-term care costs (much worse because there is no government subsidy; Medicare does not cover these expenses), and the inflationary pressures of the future.

Parting words: So do you think you can afford to retire? Determine your own CAMP score and assess your own situation honestly. I know it can be hard to do that, especially if you're really itching to leave your working life behind, but failing to examine the myriad issues associated with retirement can get you into serious trouble down the road. If the cash flow component of your CAMP score is 100 or greater, and you've got the aging, medical, and purchasing power components of your retirement plan in place, you're ready to go! Please note that CAMP score is calculated using both the cash flow and the three sustaining factors. If you retire with a cash flow equivalent to your cash flow while working but have not covered your three sustaining factors, you are not ready to retire.

You can find a quick online retirement readiness evaluation tool at www.rrralliance.com.

Golf or mah-jongg, anyone? A dip in the pool? A cruise? Or just kicking back with an umbrella drink on a Caribbean island? Sleeping in on Monday?

You got it covered!

3

Get Professional Help

TAKING THE PLUNGE INTO retirement after working throughout your adulthood is a major life decision. Deciding to retire impacts every aspect of your reality: socially, emotionally, psychologically, physically, and financially. Many men find the early days of retirement truly shocking, because their very identity was tied to their work. They simply don't know what to do with themselves, and so they follow their wives around the house like lost puppies. This can also happen to women, but to a lesser extent, because they already have a social network of friends not connected with work.

The point of these examples is to show you that retirement is more than just a financial decision, and so you need to go into it with that in mind. However, the finances will impact every other aspect of your retirement life, particularly your sense of security and contentment. All the pieces of the retirement puzzle are important, of course, but it's the money side of things that is going to make or break your so-called golden years. Retire with too little, and you set yourself up for stress and heartache. Retire with enough and with the right protections in place to guard against the inevitable adversity, and you give yourself the best shot at living out the rest of your life with as little stress and grief as possible.

If you have a physical problem, you call a doctor, right? If you have a legal problem, you call an attorney. When it comes to finances for seniors, though, figuring out whom to call for advice isn't as simple as it might sound. Really, it isn't. You certainly don't want to call Ghostbusters and trot Bill Murray and Dan Aykroyd into your living room. Your retirement isn't a laughing matter. But you might not necessarily want to call your financial adviser either. Seriously. He or she might be okay, but don't scamper blindly like a sheep. You might not like ending up with the wolves.

Pointer: Getting the right individual (or individuals) to help you plan your retirement finances and then manage them after you retire isn't as simple as it seems.

A look at your key players

Financial advisers: Unfortunately, many myths and half-truths exist in the investment world. Licensed advisers, insurance salespeople, investment brokers, and other professionals must adhere to very strict compliance standards to safeguard their clients. The best advisers develop a plan that depends on suitable investments that fit their client's needs. Lazy advisers pick the same investments for most of their clients without seriously vetting the product or considering its suitability for each individual situation. The danger of this strategy can't be overemphasized.

We live in a mega-information world, where every talking head seems to have advice they think you can use. They usually don't. Most authors and talk-show hosts promote a very simplistic, "one size fits all" approach. Tragically, seniors don't have time to recover if they take the wrong advice and their investments falter in a volatile investment world. Advisers should identify their clients' needs and find the investment solution that best fits those needs. That's often easier said than done. Few financial professionals grasp the enormous importance of focusing retirement projections on cash flow versus assets. Analyzing client information solely based upon asset accumulation can lead to a bad retirement plan that risks the quality of your retirement life.

Investment professionals typically come from business backgrounds with a focus on financial issues. Don't expect your adviser to give you good advice on taxes, insurance, reverse mortgages, Medicare, or Social Security. Your financial adviser may sell insurance as a profit maker in addition to selling investment products. While I'm not saying the adviser shouldn't sell insurance, you should get a number of opinions from insurance specialists before making a buying decision. After all, you can't be all things to all people. Many financial advisers try doing just that, and they can do a lot of financial damage to unsuspecting customers, perhaps even to customers like you.

Fee-based financial advisers: Human nature being what it is (we tend to look out for No. 1 over everything else), hiring a financial adviser to manage your investments and to advise you on other key decisions that impact on your financial health represents a viable option for some people. The adviser is usually a stockbroker earning a fee based on a percentage of the total value of your portfolio. The fee can be as high as 1 or 2 percent or more per year. You also pay other fees, such as broker commissions. The idea is that if the adviser does well for you, his or her cut will be bigger than if your portfolio drops in value. Advisers in this group will often have minimum buy-ins, meaning they require you to have a set amount of asset value before they'll represent you.

Pointer: There's a big difference between managing your assets during the accumulation stage before you retire and allocating your assets during the distribution stage. You need someone who gets the importance of cash flow versus asset retention and excess liquidity when you decide on retirement allocations. They also need a solid familiarity with both Social Security and Medicare. Unfortunately, most financial advisers do not bother to study Social Security and Medicare, because it isn't part of their sales package. Run, don't walk, from such advisers. They are salespeople, not retirement advisers.

Accountants: Accountants are good for keeping the books straight and your tax returns clear of red flags that might get the attention of the IRS. They keep up with the latest changes in the tax code, and they are bound by ethics and accepted standards. Issues such as basic tax laws, depreciation, and itemized tax deductions are right up their alley.

Few accountants have the expertise to advise you on the complex tax issues you might face during retirement: reverse mortgages, long-term care, Medicare, and Social Security. Yes, a CPA will know the basics about such things, but do you want that? I'd say no. You want more than the basics. Go to your CPA, if you have one, to get an overview. He or she can answer basic questions. Just don't take the answers and leave it at that. Find an expert with a broader background in senior-related issues. Obviously, I would say the same for most financial advisers

Tax professionals: This person might be a specialized CPA focused on seniors or a tax attorney specializing in elder clients. At the very least, you should consult with a person like this three years before you retire. Contact him or her after you've first met with your current financial adviser and CPA. Have a loose retirement strategy in mind already, and go prepared with a list of questions. You won't know all the questions to ask, so a clear indicator that you've found someone worth their salt is the number of thoughtful questions they ask you.

Here's an example of where a qualified tax adviser can help. Medical expenses for yourself, your spouse, or an elderly parent can present enormous financial strains that tax deductions can help ease. You need someone who knows how to proactively structure paying for increasing medical expenses during retirement. Deductions for medical expenses related to an elderly parent are another area where expert advice is critical. Finding a tax adviser who can advise and prepare returns correctly for complicated medical situations and deductions can be challenging. I suggest asking other experts such as tax attorneys, financial consultants, and CPAs. Interview potential candidates by asking questions about the deductibility of various expenses.

Here's a question you might ask to get a bearing on the quality of your potential tax adviser: "I expect to pay medical expenses for my parent's LTC needs. What do I have to do to be able to deduct them?"

If you do not get a confident, thoughtful answer, you haven't found the right tax professional. Move on!

Insurance specialists: Insurance specialists may focus on only one area, such as long-term care, or they may handle a broader range of insurance products that could play a part in your retirement planning and postretirement years. Don't just call your local insurance agent to talk about policies. Ask around for insurance specialists focused on seniors and retirement planning. The same goes for your financial adviser. Call a local elder-care attorney for a reference. He or she will likely be glad to provide one, and he or she might just be someone you want to talk with about your future planning as well. An insurance specialist may lack knowledge about tax laws and the finer points of reverse mortgages, Medicare, and Social Security.

A seller of long-term care products might not give you the best advice about what you should do. He or she is more likely to angle for the fat commission check. When dealing with issues of long-term care and coverage, seek out a certified long-term care specialist, not an insurance agent who happens to sell long-term care policies.

Pointer: Professionals whose entire business model is geared toward selling you a product are not generally trained to give you the comprehensive breadth of knowledge you need from your advisers. They are also inherently interested in feathering their own nests, and as a consequence, they can try to palm off products that are lucrative for them but devastating for you. As the buyer, always beware.

Community organizations: You can often get good advice from community and church organizations, at least for certain elements of your planning and ongoing retirement management. Organizations like AARP provide a treasure trove of reliable information on the Internet. Just be wary of the solicitations. Selling is the American way. Don't buy something that doesn't suit your needs.

Maybe you're thinking that calling Ghostbusters would actually be easier than finding the right combination of experts to help you. Fitting the different pieces of the puzzle together might require some legwork on your part, but the end result is you'll be receiving advice from people who know their particular area and have a focus on the needs of baby boomers planning for retirement (or who are already in retirement). You'd be surprised at how few individuals take the time to research and vet the people who give them advice, and many get burned because they didn't do their due diligence. Don't be lazy; this is your life we're talking about.

Pointer: Your experts need to collectively advise you on taxes, income, depreciation, itemized deductions, medical deductions, tax implications from asset drawdowns, Medicare, Social Security, long-term care issues and options, reverse mortgages, various insurance vehicles, investment types (including alternatives such as real estate investment trusts), and estate planning, particularly if you're married or plan to leave something to your kids.

Phew! That's a tall order. Even if you don't have all that much money, you still need at least a basic working knowledge regarding most of these topics.

What to look for in your retirement experts

The cordial handshake, the big gleaming smile, the posh office: they all can come together to give you a false sense of the person you may be trusting with your financial life. Don't let the glitz and sales schmooze get you. Go in with a realistic set of guideposts to use in your interviewing process. Here are some key things to keep in mind:

- If the expert tries to sell you a product before hearing you out in full, run!
- If the expert doesn't discuss retirement cash flow, risks such as illness requiring long-term care, comprehensive supplements to basic Medicare, and investments and other programs that increase cash flow to compensate for inflation, run!
- If the expert can't or won't supply existing customers who are planning their retirement or who are already retired as references, run!
- If the expert seems to only dabble in issues related to retirement, run!

It is critical for your expert to have your best interests in mind. You'll only get a sense of the person after you sit down with him or her for a real discussion. You might want to go in with a basic approach, just to see how the expert handles you. After the small talk, just say, "I am thinking about retiring and I don't have a clue of where to start." If you're already retired, say, "I'm already retired, but I'm not sure I've planned for what I need to. That's why I'm here." Then let the potential expert take the lead, and see where the conversation goes.

Here's a checklist of topics your potential expert should bring up:

- your intention or ability to work after you retire, or whether as a current retiree you are still working
- whether you have a corporate or government pension
- when you plan to collect Social Security, or when you began collecting it
- your past and present marital status and any negative cash flow due to dependent children or elderly parents
- retirement health care benefits from a current or former employer

- if you're retired, the nature of your supplemental Medicare coverage
- health care problems
- the nature of your assets and debts
- rental properties or other holdings that generate cash flow or will in the future

As I've noted, you will not be relying on a single expert, though you should try to find one individual to act as your primary source of information. Bring in the rest of the cast as needed.

A cautionary tale

Many of us have heard horror stories about bad investment and tax advisers. These charlatans can do real harm. Sadly, I've had to help pick up the pieces left behind after someone has been put through the financial ringer because of inappropriate advice from a supposed expert. The case below is an example of what can happen if you get lazy about finding qualified professional help for your retirement planning and management.

We'll call the unlucky lady Victoria. She got hit with bad investment and bad tax advice, and it cost her big.

Victoria's scenario

Victoria retired earlier than she planned, to care for her mother. She sacrificed her $250,000 annual income and shifted her priorities to cater to the needs of her beloved parent. During our first meeting, she lamented her terrible financial losses during two stock market downturns and a difficult divorce. Investment losses during each market downturn approached 50 percent. The first market downturn, between 2000 and 2002, hit her very hard. Her heavy exposure to technology stocks meant she felt the entire brunt of the market collapse. The technology downturn nearly wiped out Victoria's Roth IRAs. Real estate proved to be her downfall in the 2007–2009 stock market declines. Victoria and her stockbroker failed to learn the hard lessons caused by failing to properly diversify, resulting in a second round of major investment losses.

Pointer: Diversification doesn't eliminate exposure from general economic downturns (systematic risk), but it helps to greatly reduce risk from concentrated positions (nonsystematic risk). It is tempting to concentrate assets in hot companies, commodities, asset categories, or regions. However, when markets change, the losses may be dramatic and too much to bear.

Victoria experienced a critical investment phenomenon twice. Once you experience a dramatic investment loss, it's harder to restore your original position. This is because your recovery must begin from a lower investment base. Thus, if you lose half of $100,000, it takes a 100 percent gain to simply return to $100,000.

If the Investment Loss Is	Gains Required to Return to the Original Balance
20%	25%
25%	33 1/3%
33 1/3%	50%
50%	100%

Fifteen years ago, Victoria accepted a major promotion that involved transferring, so she converted her West Coast home to a rental property. Her experiences followed a pattern I frequently see. Her high income prevented her from receiving any tax benefits from deducting even the $25,000 rental loss that lower adjusted gross income (AGI; less than $100,000) taxpayers can deduct annually.

Victoria might be her new tax accountant's worst nightmare. Her income tax attributes include a "terrible trio" of unutilized investment losses. The abrupt retirement to care for her mother ended her annual

AGI stream of twenty-plus years of $200,000. When I reviewed her 2011 federal tax return, I found the following:

a. Roth IRA
   Roth market value: $180,000
   Investment basis from taxes paid on Roth IRAs: $460,000
   Unrealized Roth loss: **$280,000**

b. Taxable investment portfolio
   Market value: $520,000
   Loss carry-forwards:
       Short-term: **$170,000**
       Long-term: **$615,000**

c. Rental property
   Market value: $750,000
   Original basis: $1,100,000
   Previous depreciation: $650,000
   Net basis: $450,000
   Passive loss carry-forward: **$370,000**

d. Regular IRA: $420,000

Victoria's unused losses exceed $1,435,000. I recommended that she consider switching tax accountants. Normally, I avoid giving this advice unless I believe the current tax accountant has failed to provide appropriate service. However, Victoria's case was extreme. There were things that she could have done to save significant taxes while her income was high. Although I recommend strategies to eventually utilize most of the tax losses, the value of tax losses is best realized during high income years.

As expected, Victoria's new accountant was aghast upon discovering her plight. Her strong assets will help in planning her future, but she no longer has the income to offset losses previously realized but not effectively utilized. Fortunately, Victoria believes she can run a small consulting practice from her home while caring for her mother. She hopes to net $75,000 per year.

Pointer: Try to leverage losses during peak income years. Retirees can typically expect lower marginal tax brackets. Utilizing losses during retirement is not as effective because taxes saved pale in comparison to lost opportunities from working years.

There was a major revision in the Internal Revenue Code in 1986. Before 1986, there were only two major categories of income/losses. These two categories were:

1. Earned income from labor plus dividends and interest plus/minus rental gains/losses; no distinction was made between earned income (from work) *and* investment gains and losses from real estate investments and nonparticipative investments in businesses. These "passive" investments (from real estate and nonparticipative investments) were being used to create losses/deductions to reduce taxable income from wages and active small business ownership.

2. Capital gains/losses from investments in stocks, bonds, real estate, and other investments seeking "capital appreciation."

The pre-1986 tax code motivated taxpayers to make investments to reduce taxes, even where there was little chance of getting capital appreciation. These tax-motivated investments were frequently called "tax-sheltered" investments. The revisions in the Internal Revenue Code in 1986 created three distinct types of income/loss, with minimal opportunity to use losses from one category to offset income from another category. The three types of income are:

1. Active or earned income

2. Passive losses and gains

3. Capital gains and losses

Note that Victoria has both substantial unused passive losses and unused capital losses. Further, the ill-advised concentration in technology stocks during the technology bubble of the late 1990s resulted in massive unused Roth IRA losses. In short, Victoria's investment and tax advisers did not properly assist her during difficult economic downturns. Her advisers had failed to tell her about opportunities to minimize the pain from passive, capital, and Roth losses.

If Victoria successfully establishes her consulting practice, her new accountant and I will try to take advantage of tax losses previously realized. Victoria expected her tax accountant to provide advice in addition to preparing and filing her return. Unfortunately, this expectation is not always realized. Most tax accountants do not have the training to provide advice, and few believe they can charge enough to provide this service. I believe this is a classic problem. Good tax advice may be one of the best bargains that taxpayers can buy when their tax affairs become more complex. Retirement planning is clearly a critical time when good tax advice is needed.

What Victoria did

My first tax advice to Victoria was to totally close all her Roth IRA accounts. The IRS considers all Roth accounts as part of one Roth IRA. Thus, even though she had four losing Roth IRA accounts and one winning Roth IRA account, she needed to close all five Roth accounts in order to liquidate her Roth IRAs.

Pointer: Complete liquidation of all Roth IRAs allows a taxpayer to deduct the losses in the year of liquidation. The Roth loss deduction is taken on Schedule A as a miscellaneous itemized deduction. The loss can be offset against ordinary income. Thus, high income wage earners should absorb Roth losses when in their highest marginal tax brackets.

I suggested Victoria consider converting approximately $250,000 to $300,000 of her traditional IRA to a Roth IRA in the current year. The exact amount should be a function of her current year income plus the Roth loss available. After converting, she should collapse all of her Roth IRAs. Victoria's current year taxes will reflect both $280,000 of Roth losses and the IRA conversion income. She will pay very little federal and state taxes on the conversion, which is a good thing, especially after she lost her proverbial shirt over the last twelve years.

It is important to understand why I did not suggest Victoria convert her entire traditional IRA. Her traditional IRA accounts substantially exceed her available Roth loss. It would not be prudent for her to convert the excess traditional IRA in the same year she recognizes the Roth loss. She should spread the conversion of her remaining traditional IRA as appropriate in future years. It is very likely that some portion of her traditional IRA will never be converted.

Between retirement contributions and Roth losses realized, we will attempt to minimize any taxes Victoria owes on her current year consulting income. However, we can't offset employment taxes on her earned income.

Parting words: Victoria's example strays into the somewhat complex and arcane world of tax law, but it shows just how important it is to get advice, even if you don't totally get what was going on in her story. Good financial management in the accumulation and distribution stages is critical. Many of us did not get the advice we needed, and so losses for small investors in the last twelve years have been astounding. Lives have been ruined, and retirements have been exploded or deferred, perhaps permanently. Having experts in your corner won't guarantee that everything will be just peachy, but making the effort to find the best possible people to stand with you in the trenches will go a long way to reducing your overall risk when the markets head south again. And believe me, they will. It's only a matter of time. Proper risk management and financial planning requires the deft hand of experts. Make sure to find and work with the right ones for you.

4

Your Skin in the Game

WHEN IT COMES DOWN to brass tacks about retirement talk, assets walk the walk. Without them, you can't retire. It's as simple as that. Social Security is an asset, and it's more valuable than most people think. A pension is an asset. Most people who have one know it and thank their lucky stars that they've got it. Your house is an asset too. If you've got sufficient equity in your home and aren't upside down on your mortgage, you can use that equity to generate cash flow. While that's not always smart, sometimes it is. Or you could move out and rent the house, but then you need someplace else to live. Obviously, the usual suspects like savings accounts, certificates of deposit, money market accounts, stocks, mutual funds, individual retirement accounts (IRAs), 401(k)s, self-employment pensions (SEPs), bonds, whole-life insurance policies, rental properties or other forms of real estate, equity in a business, ownership of a business, jewels, rare coins, a chest of pirate treasure, and the Holy Grail are all (or could be, maybe, in the case of the pirate stash or the Holy Grail) assets that go together to form your net worth after you subtract how much debt you have.

As I said earlier, you are an asset as well. Your skills and talents are worth money. Otherwise, you wouldn't have been working in the first place. Don't forget the "you" factor when you start counting up the assets you have as you plan your retirement or reevaluate your current retirement situation. Work pays. Assets pay, or they should. I'll beat the cash flow drum later, in a short time, in fact, but before I do, it's important to sum up the various traditional investment vehicles that many of us use to build wealth and generate cash flow before and after we retire.

Some of my explanations are going to be obvious to you. Others will hopefully tantalize you and inspire you to delve deeper. Suffice it to say that there are scads of books out there on investments and investment strategies. I don't intend to duplicate that information here. I'm not going to get into short-selling stocks or the absolute peril of buying on margin. I'm not going to get into the wonders of investing in pork bellies (commodities). Part of your education should include boning up on investment vehicles, especially securities (stocks). You need to know what's out there so you can make informed decisions. When you buy a refrigerator, flat-screen TV, or car, don't you check out the findings in *Consumer Reports*? I hope so. So doesn't it make sense to learn as much as you can about the investments you make that will help you pay the light bill after you punch out from work on a permanent basis? In my more than forty years in finance and from my days as an active licensed financial planner, I have been amazed at how many people don't take the time to understand the power of their money. Take responsibility for it. Believe me, nobody cares about it as much as you do.

So let's get on with the basics of investments, and then I'll get into the retirement cash flow philosophy that is so integral to the foundation of this retirement planning and management book.

Savings accounts

In the United States, savings accounts receive the backing of the Federal Deposit Insurance Corporation (FDIC) for owners of a single account, per bank, up to $250,000. Due to historic lows in interest rates, hiding the cash in your mattress yielded about the same returns as most banks. The good thing is your money was safe and liquid. The bad thing is inflation gnawed at its value. In early 2013, the top banks were paying a staggeringly low 0.15 percent, or annual interest of $1,500 on a savings account worth $1 million!

Certificates of deposit

In the United States, certificate of deposit accounts receive backing by the Federal Deposit Insurance Corporation for owners of a single account, per bank, up to $250,000. The time frame or the investment period for certificates of deposit has typically varied from three months to five years. Interest rates grew from less than 2 percent in the early 1950s to as much as 15 percent in the early 1980s. However, most seniors learned to expect 4 to 7 percent per year interest during the last twenty years. Rapidly declining interest (both cost to borrowers and return to investors) has made this simple and safe investment type less useful to retirees.

> Traditional CDs have paid slightly more interest than savings accounts. In early 2013, the highest competitive rate for a one-year CD was just south of 1 percent. Most one-year CDs were paying about 0.45 percent, or $450 per year on an investment of $100,000. Five-year CDs ranged from 1.0 to a high of 1.5 percent, meaning you'd get a return of practically nothing in exchange for locking up your money for half a decade. A CD is not a liquid asset, which can be a downside if you suddenly need cash.

Pointer: Odd terms (e.g., eleven or thirteen months) for smaller financial institutions often pay more than standard six-month or one-year CDs. These institutions may be seeking bank reserves to balance a lending opportunity. Larger institutions don't have to offer the same good deals because of their size and economies of scale.

Money market accounts

Money market accounts work in different ways, and not all of them are backed by the FDIC, which means there's some risk to some of them.

In other words, you can lose principal if a bank goes bust. In early 2013, the best rates from top banks for money market accounts were between 0.75 and 0.9 percent per year, with no minimum balance and low fees. If you kept $100,000 in a money market, the best you could hope for would be a return of $900 per year. If you had $1 million tied up in a money market, you'd have a staggering $9,000 to play with. Money markets are usually liquid, but some have restrictions on the number of withdrawals you can make in a given time period. Others have minimum balance requirements and high fees.

> It's no surprise that seniors have been pulling their hair out. The historic low interest rates of recent years have rightfully been called a "drive-by shooting" of senior citizens in terms of their ability to fund their retirements in less risky investment tools that provide enough of a return to keep the lights on. As a consequence, many seniors have felt forced to put their money into far more risky investments, such as stocks and mutual funds. Some seniors have lost most of what they have, while others have done okay, and some have done rather well. Money markets are liquid, and they've all lost value of principal due to inflation.

Bonds

Bonds have been a good deal in recent years because of the historically low interest rates. Government, municipal, and corporate bonds all have different sets of risk and benefits. The key thing about bonds is that you know how much interest you'll get on your investment, when the interest will be paid, and when you'll get your principal back (as long as the company you invested in doesn't go belly up). The attraction of US-backed bonds is that Uncle Sam isn't likely to leave town anytime soon. Municipal bonds were once thought to be relatively safe, but nowadays I'd advise the shopper to be very careful.

When you buy a bond, you're buying debt, which isn't such a bad thing if you know the debtor is good for the tab. Let's say the company Bo's Dog Treats Inc. wanted to raise $100 and market conditions ruled that the company needs a "coupon rate" (interest rate) of 6 percent to get banks, bond funds, and individual investors to climb aboard. Each bond would typically be $1,000 (known as par value), generating $60 of income per year. Bo's Dog Treats Inc. would agree to pay back the $1,000 in 2023. In other words, the bond would mature in ten years and would pay you $60 per year over the lifetime of the bond. Sounds cool, right? It actually is, at least in theory. Bonds have been the best friend of retirees for decades, because they're simple, they're relatively safe, and they usually offered excellent annual returns people put toward their cash flow to pay bills.

Here's the rub: If Bo's Dog Treats Inc. hits the skids, then the risk of owning its bonds goes up. That in turn means if you sell your Bo's Dog Treats Inc. bond, you'll have to offer the buyer a higher interest rate than the 6 percent Bo's Dog Treats Inc. has agreed to pay. To make up the difference, the buyer will want to pay less than the par value of the bond. In other words, that nice, warm, and fuzzy Bo's Dog Treats Inc. bond you thought was so great when you bought it is now worth $800 instead of $1,000. Yikes! It's great for the buyer, though, because the overall yield on the bond will be higher than it was for you. The buyer would have paid less for the bond, making money on it, and he or she would still get the 6 percent annual return Bo has agreed to pay.

Hikes in prevailing interest rates over time can also erode the value of Bo's Dog Treats Inc.'s bond. If the prevailing rate rises to 7 percent, then buyers won't want Bo's Dog Treats Inc.'s bonds. To sell you'd have to offer the bond at a lower price than you paid.

Bond mutual funds are in the business of playing the bond game, and they allow you to get in on the action with relatively low investments, which isn't always possible when individuals of modest means attempt to jump into the bond market on their own. Bond funds buy a basket of bonds from various entities and try to play the bond market, timing buying and selling as conditions in the market dictate. The problem is that these funds can (and do) go down when interest rates rise. In early 2013, with interest rates at a near record low, a ten-year Treasury note was yielding about 2 percent. Again, not so great, eh? Other bonds pay higher yields, but you have to accept the increased risk that goes along with the higher return on the investment.

In early 2013, two major brokerage houses informed clients heavily invested in bonds that they were being reclassified as aggressive investors. The rationale for this reclassification was the price behavior of bonds. I recommend bond investors invest only in bonds they are prepared to hold to maturity. If held to maturity, there is little risk of loss of principal, and the annual cash flow is known. However, investors in bond funds do not have the same low risk that buy-and-hold bond investors have with individual bonds. Individual bonds mature. Bond funds typically maintain the same average time to maturity for their lifetime. Thus, if interest rates have risen during the holding period for a bond fund, the investor should receive capital losses. However, if interest rates are down during the investor's holding period, the investor will realize capital gains. Many readers will think I have reversed gains and losses. Remember that interest rates and bond prices move in opposite directions. Thus, rising interest rates cause bond investors to lose value.

Stocks

Stocks are part of the financial lexicon. Basically, a stock is a share in a publicly traded company. You own a piece of the company when you buy a share of stock. Some stocks pay dividends (more on that later), and others don't. Simple, right? Actually, it is simple. However, there are all kinds of stocks from all kinds of companies, each with their own attendant risks in a given sector of the overall market. You've got small-cap, mid-cap, and large-cap stocks, meaning you're buying shares in small, medium, and large companies, respectively. There are different market sectors like financials, biotech, and information technology.

Let's go with some more basics here. The Dow Jones Industrial Average is comprised of the nation's thirty largest companies. These are known as blue-chip stocks. The National Association of Securities Dealers Automated Quotations, now commonly known as the NASDAQ stock exchange, comprises more than five thousand of the most actively traded over-the-counter stocks in the American Stock Exchange. The Standard & Poor's 500, or S&P 500, is a basket of five hundred of the most widely held stocks, mostly mid- and large-cap companies.

Established in 1957, the S&P 500 index is supposed to reflect the performance of the stock market as a whole. People trust the S&P 500, so what it's doing at any given moment is worth taking into account. The Dow is a reflection of the blue chips. The tiny membership pool in the elite Dow club means that if one or two of the big boys goes south on any given day, the Dow will take a hit. That doesn't mean your stocks went down, it just means that the Dow went down. The NASDAQ and the S&P 500 will give you a better picture of what's going on. So don't freak if the Dow goes down. It does all the time, as you well know. Do get concerned if you see all three of these players take a dive off the high board, but don't panic and sell with the rest of the herd. I always advise my clients to pick the best stocks they can and stick with them, unless disturbing trends emerge in a given sector or with a particular company.

Mutual funds

Mutual funds were once thought to be safe bets for small investors. In many ways, they still are, but anyone who has been in mutual funds since the late 1990s knows all too well that "safe" is definitely a relative term. A mutual fund was supposed to be safe because the fund holds a large basket of companies. Sector mutual funds hold a smaller basket of companies in the same industry. If you jumped into IT sector mutual funds in the dot.com crazy days of the late 1990s, only to see your investment tank, raise your hand; many of us got burned in the dot.com bubble. We saw our investments soar to phenomenal highs. Returns of 25 percent were considered meager. People thought they could double their money in a few years. The point is that mutual funds are simply baskets of companies, and supposedly provide a little safety in numbers. The thinking is, if a few bad apples show up in the basket, the good apples will take up the slack.

Sadly, that hasn't been true during the last two financial meltdowns. The bad apples infected all the good apples too. Many people lost their shirts in mutual funds. While I don't necessarily steer my clients away from mutual funds, I do think buying dividend-paying blue-chip stocks (stocks that pay a percentage on shares to shareholders every year) are a better bet from a cash flow point of view. With a dividend-paying stock (or bond, for that matter), you can build cash flow that you can count on during your retirement. You can buy mutual funds that pay a dividend too, of course.

A few words on dollar-cost averaging

If you've been in the stock market in individual stocks or in mutual funds, chances are your financial adviser has urged you to do dollar-cost averaging. The theory is, you set up a regular schedule to buy into your basket of securities, be they individual stocks or mutual funds, as a way of building your portfolio without the temptation to time the market. The theory also goes that if you are a disciplined investor, you'll keep buying when the market is low. The idea is that over time, when you buy low, the value gained will offset the losses when you bought high, averaging everything out rather nicely.

Sounds great, right? Well, not so fast. Dollar-cost averaging protects investors in the stock market during the accumulation stage. It increases investor returns over the reported average rate of return for the period. As I've said, this occurs because investment discipline allows the investor to buy more units when the price is low and fewer when the price is high. The technique provides the discipline. Investors do not have to decide when to buy; they simply invest the same fixed amount each year.

Pointer: During the distribution stage of retirement, dollar-cost averaging is generally disastrous for investors. When prices are low, they have to sell more units to get the same distribution. Buy high/sell low doesn't work!

A few words on portfolio diversification

Diversified portfolios do *not* guarantee either better investment performance or less portfolio volatility. However, diversified portfolios increase the potential for maximizing expected return for a given level of risk. Retirees should always contemplate whether their cash flow needs are being met. Taking more investment risk *may* be necessary to meet cash flow needs.

Bear in mind, though, that nondiversified investments have the potential to score tremendous investment returns for you. In other words, if you put all your eggs in a nest that seems to be home for the Golden Goose, you can make a boatload of cash. Remember the tech sector funds of the dot.com bubble? Don't be tempted. If these so-called bonanza investments do not do well, they will affect your quality of life.

Pointer: The cost of an investment should never be judged in a vacuum. Costs should always be viewed against benefits. So if it costs a little more to buy into a particular investment that serves your needs and suits your risk level, you must weigh the benefits to you against the costs of the buy-in.

The two most important questions for choosing investment products are needs and suitability. Unfortunately, many writers, talk-show hosts, and regulators focus on liquidity and costs. The ideal retirement investment produces substantial cash flow with little (or no) risk of loss of principal. Some degree of liquidity can more easily be sacrificed if there is no need for using principal to meet cash flow needs. That's something to keep in mind when choosing investments and when planning your retirement strategy. A bond, which should not be considered a liquid asset, may be the right choice because the risk is low and the return will generate the cash flow you need.

A few words on IRAs, 401(k)s, and Roth IRAs

When you earn money, the government grabs its share. Obviously, you know that. You also know that it's a very nice thing indeed to not pay federal income taxes on as much income as possible. To give you an incentive to save for your retirement, Uncle Sam has set up the individual retirement account and the 401(k) programs. Self-employed individuals can set up a self-employment pension, which is basically a 401(k) for all intents and purposes.

The beauty of a 401(k) is that your employer kicks in a contribution, sometimes even matching your contributions dollar-for-dollar. In an SEP, you're paying for your own retirement with no outside help from an employer. It's a bit more complicated, but that's about the size of it.

In general, these three programs allow you to reduce your overall federal income tax liabilities through your contributions, meaning you take a cut off the top that lowers your adjusted gross income. In the financial world, these investment vehicles are called qualified investments. Conversely, a nonqualified investment is one purchased with money you've already paid taxes on, and one that you pay taxes on when the principal grows.

Pointer: Income taxes are deferred on the money you make and contribute to qualified investment accounts like IRAs and 401(k)s during high-earning years. When you take distributions from these accounts after reaching the minimum age of fifty-nine and a half, your distributions are taxed as ordinary income. The idea is that you will be in a lower tax bracket when you retire, so you'll pay a lower rate of income tax. The other bonus is that in making the contribution, you've lowered the gross amount you would have been taxed on in a higher tax bracket during your peak earning years.

It makes good sense to lower your adjusted gross income in high earning years by deferring taxes on the income you set aside for your retirement until you actually spend the tax-deferred funds. I'm frequently amazed at how many people don't set up an IRA or a 401(k) in spite of the obvious financial advantages of doing so. If you're a boomer and haven't set up an IRA or a 401(k), or you haven't adopted a disciplined contribution schedule, then you're missing the proverbial boat on two of the best retirement cash flow options you've got going for you at the moment.

If you can defer $6,000 of income from taxes during a given year of your work life, you can invest the full $6,000 in your IRA or 401(k) and build it from there. If you take the six grand, you pay income taxes on more money than you would have had to pay, and you'd be left with only $4,800 of that $6,000 to invest or spend. So failing to defer cost you $1,200, depending on your income and tax bracket. Regardless of how much you make, the concept remains the same. Defer income taxes and sock as much tax-deferred money away as you can, and don't stop funding these accounts in the years just before you retire. That's when you should be going great guns, not pulling back.

Roth IRAs

Uncle Sam has gone one step further to help you prepare for your retirement years. As part of the Taxpayer Relief Act of 1997, the old gent established the Roth IRA program, which is a fantastic opportunity. Your contributions are made from your after-tax income, but later withdrawals (distributions) are not subject to federal income taxes, though certain rules do apply. You also don't pay income taxes on the growth of the funds in the account, whereas in a taxable stock account, for example, you'd have to pay tax on dividends and capital gains. Contribution levels are dependent on your age, income, and income tax filing status. Unlike with a traditional IRA or 401(k), you don't have to start taking distributions at age seventy and a half, and you can even use up to $10,000 of your Roth IRA to make a first-time home purchase.

When Roth IRA contributions make the most sense

- When income is low for a given year, it may be a good year to make a Roth IRA contribution to allow all future earnings to be nontaxable on that account. The point is, you won't need the tax break from a traditional IRA, SEP, or 401(k) to lower your gross taxable income as much, so you can more easily afford to take after-tax dollars and plunk them down in a Roth because of the future payoff.
- Roth distributions are not a part of the calculation of the taxability of Social Security benefits. Thus, some retirees may pay less Social Security taxes by withdrawing from a Roth IRA for retirement needs first.

To illustrate:

Social Security benefits are taxable if the benefits cause the taxpayer's income to exceed a threshold. Current tax rules for Social Security benefits begin taxation at $25,000 of modified adjusted gross income (MAGI) for single taxpayers and $32,000 for married taxpayers. One-half of Social Security benefits are includible in the MAGI calculation.

You can convert a traditional IRA to a Roth IRA by electing to pay the taxes at a chosen point in return for no future taxes. The advantage of Roth IRAs is that a taxpayer elects to pay taxes in a low tax year to eliminate taxes when the taxpayer's income is higher. Senior taxpayers with little or no income should either convert their IRAs to a Roth IRA, or draw them down first to pay medical expenses. They will incur either no tax or much less tax than their heirs would incur if they inherit a taxable IRA.

So you see, it is often wise for a low income taxpayer to convert a small IRA prior to retirement to a Roth IRA. The distribution from a Roth IRA is not includible in the calculation of the taxability of Social Security, but distributions from a traditional IRA are. By making the conversion prior to receiving Social Security, the taxpayer may save a lot of total taxes.

Roth IRAs provide an excellent means for reducing tax levels during the key withdrawal period after retirement. Since the nontaxable status is preserved for those who inherit the Roth account, they also provide a great asset to pass to heirs. A comprehensive analysis should be made to decide whether to make Roth conversions.

Roth IRAs work best when long periods of tax-free growth follow their creation. A minimum of five years should be allotted for growth. It is seldom advisable to create Roths for immediate use. Unfortunately, even the most tax-oriented CPAs do not fully understand Roth principles. Many taxpayers and their advisers neglect to fund a Roth IRA (or convert existing funds to a Roth IRA), and the missed opportunity may be huge.

Pointer: Plan and manage your retirement through selecting investments that are most likely to produce and increase cash flow over time, to guard against the erosive effects of inflation. Retirees should place greater emphasis on cash flow than stock appreciation. Cash flow is more reliable and pays the bills in the near term.

Parting words: As you can see, the world of investing in traditional vehicles can be quite complicated indeed. However, despite certain decades where the stock market provided low or no returns, over time, well-chosen stocks have historically returned more than other "safer" investments. Even if you've been burned twice in the last decade or so, don't turn your back completely on stocks and bonds. Both have a place in your retirement preparations and in providing you with cash flow after you retire. That said, I do not recommend relying only on equities for cash flow during your golden years. More creative approaches are needed. As I've said, an excessive emphasis on asset accumulation and retention before and during retirement sells you short in the end. Cash flow is king!

5

Alternative Investments Aren't a Hail Mary

IN RECENT YEARS, INVESTORS have been looking for a better way to gain returns on their money. For we retirees, the decline in interest rates and the volatility of the stock market has prompted us to join the hunt. We're taking a closer look at things such as annuities, which aren't really alternative investments, per se, and real estate investment trusts (REITs), which most assuredly are. There are also a number of other ways to put your money to work that would fit nicely into the "think outside of the box" equation in today's brave new world of investing for retirement.

Pension and Benefits magazine reported that in 2003, $15.4 billion was invested in alternative investments (not stocks and bonds). By 2011, they reported that $94.6 billion of new money was invested in alternative investments. This represents over a 500 percent increase. By contrast, in 2011, they reported that only $65.9 billion of new money was invested in stocks and bonds. The primary attraction of alternative investments such as REITs is cash flow. Many REITs have annual income of 6 percent. Senior investors seeking cash flow frequently find stocks too risky and bonds paying too little cash flow. They find the high income cash flow of REITs very attractive.

Many advisers have replaced bond allocations with allocations to alternative investments. Seniors needing cash flow frequently sacrifice liquidity (alternative investments are typically not as liquid as bonds or bond funds) for the significantly higher cash flows that alternative investments provide. Since current interest rates are at the lowest level since the 1930s and the cash flow from bonds is poor, it is not surprising that there is a net exodus from bond funds and a rapid increase in alternative investing. Morningstar reports that 65 percent of advisers and 67 percent of institutions say alternatives are "as important as or more important than traditional investments."

Investment News Survey shows that real estate investment trusts represent almost 25 percent of alternative investments. Commodities are another 12 percent of alternatives. As noted, the attraction is higher cash flow than bonds and less volatility than with stock funds. Variable annuities with living benefits provide another possible source of much higher cash flow without the volatility stocks have experienced between 2000 and 2013 and the potential risks of bond funds as interest rates rise in the next few years. Variable annuities can offer a combination of guaranteed cash flow with the potential for principal growth if the stock market performs well. It is very common for 50 percent of a senior investor's assets to be invested in a combination of alternatives and variable annuities with living benefits. This combination provides cash flow with upside potential.

A word to the skeptics: New financial vehicles are frequently viewed as too risky and complex when first introduced. Within a few years, study and experience may show they fit an investor need. Niche investments generally arise because there is a need. Many new investments would have been accepted and utilized more quickly if the financial press and financial advisers were focused more on cash flow and less on liquidity.

Many financial columnists and talk-show hosts view annuities as bad investments. Prior to the last ten years, this belief was usually correct. However, changes in products and a decade of poor mutual fund performance have changed things dramatically. The disappearance of employer pensions has resulted in seniors needing "personal pension" replacements. Investors may be well advised to protect future income by utilizing a variable annuity to ensure a minimal monthly cash flow. I caution that annuities should not be your only retirement investment. Select annuities may be appropriate where no employer pension exists. All income and assets should be considered prior to selecting an annuity or investing in a REIT.

Let's get into some real detail here on annuities and REITs. If I were a betting man, I'd wager you haven't thought much about either option. Don't worry. You're not alone. As I said, annuities have gotten a bad rap, and the stigma lingers, and after the recent nuclear blast in the real estate market, it's no surprise that lots of folks get jittery at the mere mention of investments related to real estate. Keep an open mind, though. You might be surprised at what you learn.

Annuities (fixed and variable)

An annuity is a life insurance product designed to provide lifetime income to the owner. You, the owner, pick select investments (like specified mutual funds) to power the growth of the annuity. Your annuity policy may be fixed (the value increases annually based on an interest component) or variable (the value is determined by mutual fund performance). A fixed annuity pays an annual income for the life of the individual. There will typically be a residual value for the heirs of the participant. Variable annuities typically pay an income based upon the greater of original value or a higher value determined by growth in the underlying invest.

A key feature that a high percentage of annuities now have is called a living benefit. Policies with living benefits may guarantee increased income for each year that no distributions are made. Living benefits are an insurance company's promise to pay income off the greater of current market value or a higher market value achieved during the term of the annuity (sometime highest daily value, or highest quarterly value, or highest annual value). There is also frequently a guarantee that income grows by 4 to 6 percent per year during the period of deferral, even if the market declines.

Annuities with living benefits generally provide a growing guaranteed future income base but do not guarantee future asset values. Investors should fully utilize the insurance company promise they pay for. This means they should do the following:

1. Invest aggressively, because if the investment does not perform, then income will be based upon the minimum guaranteed growth.

2. Do *not* diversify. Each chosen investment should stand on its own. The income guarantees protect against the lack of diversification.

3. Select initial bonuses offered if they are part of the guaranteed growth.

Annuities traditionally involved trading a lump sum for a guaranteed payment for life. The classic illustration was when a beneficiary of a life insurance policy was given a choice between a lump sum and a guaranteed monthly (or annual) income for life. The traditional annuity gave individuals the opportunity to insure that they had an income they couldn't outlive, but frankly the loss of potential growth appeared greater during the period 1980–2000, when earning rates were good to excellent on almost all asset classes. In other words, buying a fixed or variable annuity during this period wasn't considered a great idea.

Now, however, the annuity equation is changing fast. For example, variable annuities with living benefit riders have two parts: an income part and an investment part. As noted, income is typically guaranteed based upon the original investment plus a guaranteed increase per year. However, the guaranteed income increase per year is typically terminated once withdrawals begin. After withdrawals begin, increases only occur if the investment growth exceeds withdrawals. During the deferral stage, investment market increases may exceed the guaranteed rate of increase. This would result in the insurance company crediting the insured with the higher market increase. The bottom line is, the base for computing income can only remain the same or increase based upon the higher of the guaranteed increase in the income base or the market base (generally a chosen basket of mutual funds), less 3 to 4 percent for insurance company costs. The key is to buy the annuity features that meet your need.

As noted, from 2000 to the present, annuity contracts have improved dramatically. Most contracts today do not require individuals to give up control of the assets (they don't promise to give up the control of the assets in return for the insurance company's promise to pay future benefits). There is thus an opportunity for individuals to participate in stock market appreciation without risking income based upon original investment.

To illustrate:

Assume Sarah Jones invests $20,000 on January 15, 2013. On March 20, the investment has grown to $21,100. On April 15, the investment value is $20,500.

An insurance company basing income on the highest daily value might pay 5 percent at age sixty-five on $21,100 (the highest daily value). By contrast, an insurance company paying income on the highest quarterly value would pay income on $20,500.

Annuities play a critical role in helping give individuals an opportunity to grow their income without sacrificing cash flow if the stock market does poorly. Thus, in our cash flow approach, we will typically recommend an annuity if guaranteed income is inadequate to meet monthly need. The downside risk is minimized for the individual who can't afford to bear the risk of the market.

Obviously, there is a cost for the insurance company bearing the downside risk of the market and giving the investor upside potential. The typical cost for annuity features is 3 to 4 percent per year. This cost seems really high, but one must remember that this cost typically comes out of the upside only. If the insurance company guarantees an increase of 5 percent per year in income (during the deferral period), even if the market goes down, then the 3 to 4 percent plays a role only in the investor getting more than 5 percent per year increase (i.e., 9.5 percent stock return – 4.0 percent costs), resulting in 5.5 percent increase in income, or 0.5 percent more than the guaranteed increase. Only under unusual circumstances would I ever recommend switching a good existing annuity. The benefits of the new policy must greatly exceed the existing policy. Costs related to surrender and acquisition of a new policy generally make the exchange inadvisable.

A variable annuity with living benefits costs covers all of the following:

- risk premium to the insurance company for "guaranteeing" future cash flows based upon an income base that may increase if the underlying mutual funds appreciate but can never decrease
- mutual fund costs
- insurance company administrative costs

When a financial need arises, solutions emerge that meet that need. Variable annuities with living benefits fill a senior's need for regular reliable cash flow during retirement. They give seniors some opportunity to participate in market gains without risking their cash flow. Purchasing power risk is mitigated by the potential for increasing (but not decreasing) income. Variable annuities with living benefits provide retirement cash flow, but at a cost. Insurance companies provide downside protection in some combination of the following ways:

- Consistent cash flows that can grow but never decrease are promised.

- Investors are insured against loss of principal. Principal can grow but not decrease.
- Investors can share in investment gains.

The costs are the following:

- Investor gains may be capped (no more than an upside limit).
- Investors share in gains but only if the excess of market gains over guaranteed rates is more than 4 percent.
- Example: The underlying mutual fund goes up 14 percent. The investor income base is guaranteed to grow 5 percent if no withdrawals are made that year. The insurance company costs and profits total 4.25 percent. The investor gets 4.75 percent plus their cash flow (if they draw the 5 percent) or 9.75 percent if they defer cash flow.

Remember, investment choices are limited to select mutual funds to prevent excess insurance company exposure. There are many nuances and complexities in variable annuity policies. Expert advice is advised prior to purchasing a variable annuity.

Pointer: I suggest you never invest more than 30 percent of your assets in a variable annuity. Also, you should only replace an annuity if there are no surrender charges on the old policy, or the new policy has far more financial advantages.

Getting to know REITs

Before I get into the nitty-gritty on real estate investment trusts and a couple other alternative investments, keep in mind that you should evaluate any investment based on the following four general rules of thumb:

1. Current and future income stream

2. Term or life

3. Liquidation value

4. Risk of loss of income and principal (liquidation value)

Obviously, some forms of investment are easier to evaluate on the above points than others. When it comes to REITs, these four rules should be kept firmly in mind. Now, let's get on with the discussion on REITs.

Real estate investment trusts are corporate entities that invest in real estate. REITs eliminate corporate tax and are required to distribute 90 percent of their taxable income to investors. The investors are responsible for paying taxes on their share of the income. The REIT structure is designed to provide a real estate investment structure similar to the structure mutual funds provide for investment in stocks.

Most future and present retirees think they have to rely on government bonds, corporate bonds, and certificates of deposit for income, along with dividends from stocks or profits taken off the top of principal invested in stocks and mutual funds when gains occur. Current annual returns from nearly all of the traditional income sources are less than 5 percent, and many of these investments produce cash flow less than 2 percent per year. Carefully selected REITs, such as student housing partnerships, may provide attractive income alternatives. A major trade-off for greater income is reduced liquidity. Many investors and advisers attach too much weight to liquidity; they focus almost entirely on asset accumulation and fail to appreciate the needs of seniors for regular cash flow. That's why I think looking into REITs might be a great option.

Institutional investors responded quickly to major income shifts in the market, but seniors and their advisers react more cautiously to changing investment environments. REITs, student housing, and other income investments with three- to seven-year liquidity restrictions have a place in planning for your retirement. These real estate niche investments are demographically sound and may provide income of 5 to 8 percent per year, *with* upside potential. Thus, they may provide both current cash flow and potential for increasing future income (meeting purchasing power and inflation concerns).

Including REITs in a retirement portfolio provides excellent income, provides income growth to increase purchasing power, and may provide diversification. REIT elements include equity like growth potential and fixed income. The combined effect can reduce risk and provide income protection. REIT investments may be either publicly traded or nontraded. Traded REITs market exposure balance the negative of market exposure with the advantage of liquidity. Nontraded REITs lack liquidity but limit market exposure.

I generally prefer the limited liquidity, higher income, greater capital gain potential, and most importantly reduced sequence risk (poor returns earlier in retirement that drain assets) of nontraded REITs for my clients. Some nontraded REITs give exposure to unique niches of real estate. Among my favorite niches are self-storage REITs, industrial REITs, student housing REITs, and health care REITs. However, there are other REIT types where public REITs are both available and good, for example, apartment REITs. I generally feel that the excess yield and greater value in public nontraded REITs compensate for liquidity disadvantages versus listed REITs in the same category.

Nontraded REITs and variable annuities are both classic examples of investments that can be very useful sources of retirement cash flows. A recent Jane Bryant Quinn article in the *AARP Monthly News Bulletin* did an excellent job describing "variable annuities with living benefits." She begins by saying, "I know what you want in a retirement investment: terrific stock market gains without any risk of loss and a steady stream of retirement income."

Bryant Quinn contributes regularly to *AARP Bulletin* and other financial publications. She has earned a reputation as a tough but open-minded financial columnist. Although she suggests there are no such dreamy products, she identifies candidates. One candidate identified is a variable annuity with living benefits. Income continues for life with potential increases for stock market gains and deferring the start of receiving benefits.

A few words on self-storage stocks

According to Yahoo Finance, the largest listed self-storage is Public Storage, which appreciated almost 3,200 percent from January 1, 1988, until September 1, 2012. Extra Space Storage is the second largest segment of self-storage stocks. Over the last five years, as of September 1, 2012, both were up over 100 percent in a period when the widely followed Standard & Poor's 500 stock index was slightly negative. Self-storage has proven a great industry in both good and bad economic conditions. Over the last twenty-five years, self-storage stocks have substantially outperformed the S&P 500 Index. So if you haven't considered this sector as an area for investment, give it some thought.

Pointer: Constructing a retirement portfolio requires balancing growth, income, and liquidity and minimizing sequence risk (poor returns early on in retirement that decrease your asset base).

A few words on alternative mutual funds, gold, and the kitchen sink

Alternative asset mutual funds don't provide substantial income, but their upside potential and diversification benefits both reduce sequence risk and purchasing power risk for retirees. I suggest a small allocation for retiree portfolios. I do caution, however, against the tendency of some advisers to allocate too much to gold in retirement portfolios. Gold is not an industrial metal. Thus, its primary value is tied to hedging against inflation and volatility. Other investment vehicles besides REITs and alternative asset mutual funds that may provide both the required income maintenance and increased income to offset purchasing power costs include equity indexed annuities and Treasury inflation-protected securities (TIPSs).

Equity indexed annuities: I confess to disliking equity indexed annuities, but I grudgingly admit they do provide potential to protect current income, while providing limited potential for increased income. Equity indexed annuities are insurance products that guarantee no reduction in underlying investment value in years where equity indexes are negative (the investment is credited with zero return or a contractually guaranteed return for that year), but limit very substantially equity returns in positive equity years. Features I dislike are little upside potential, very high internal costs (selling advisers typically receive a 10 to 15 percent commission), and long-term withdrawal charges.

Treasury inflation-protected securities: TIPSs were championed by Secretary of Treasury Robert Rubin. These securities earned a specified rate of return plus the annual rate of inflation. They remain a great idea conceptually, but their utility has been limited by low inflation and low interest rates in recent years.

Energy master limited partnerships (MLPs): An MLP is an enterprise that engages in certain businesses, generally related to the use of natural resources. This includes all manner of activities related to producing, processing, or transporting oil, natural gas, and coal. These MLPs trade on securities exchanges like a stock. Their income frequently averages between 6 and 10 percent.

MLPs are taxed as partnerships, avoiding corporate taxes, and pay a greater distribution than REITs and utilities. Because MLPs trade on a listed exchange, they are highly liquid.

Parting words: Regular, steady cash flow is really just a form of an annuity or pension. The new (since approximately 2003) generation of variable annuities with living benefits provide this cash flow, with the potential for increasing income if the stock market does well. REITs may provide the cash flow but may not have the downside protection. Alternative investments should figure into your retirement package. Give some thought to how you can make annuities and REITs meet your cash flow needs, and always seek advice from an expert familiar with these sorts of investments.

6

Social Security and You

IN THE PAST, THERE was no safety net for senior citizens. They worked until they dropped, or they lived with relatives until the Grim Reaper showed up to collect them. Those without families to support them in old age frequently found themselves homeless and starving. It wasn't a pretty picture. The plight of the elderly became even worse during the Great Depression in the 1930s. As part of Franklin D. Roosevelt's New Deal, Congress passed the Social Security Act of 1935, establishing the program we all know and rely on today. Its core concept was to allow us to pay into a national retirement plan while we were working and then to collect benefits to help us make ends meet in our old age, when we could no longer work.

Big changes are afoot in the near future, though, and the safety net we once thought we could count on could be weakened in an effort to whittle down the national budget deficit and to pay down the national debt. We've all heard how the waves of baby boomers that started hitting the beach in 2011 are going to stretch Social Security to the limit in coming years. The system is solvent now, but it might not be in the future. In today's hostile economy, Social Security is all that's keeping some seniors afloat. Younger baby boomers would be wise to build and manage their own assets to protect themselves against any changes Congress might make in Social Security, like drastically increasing the full retirement age (the present age is sixty-six). Sadly, there may well come a day when the elderly are set adrift and left to largely fend for themselves, or the burden will increasingly fall on families as harsh economic times continue.

For those of us who are either already at full retirement age or approaching it, the importance of taking full advantage of all the benefits available from the Social Security program cannot be overemphasized. Social Security is probably the most valuable and powerful financial tool you have, especially if you are of modest means and possess limited assets. In order to effectively make decisions about how Social Security can help you, you need a basic understanding of the program's nuts and bolts. In addition, I strongly recommend that you consult with an adviser with a solid background in Social Security before you make any decision about collecting benefits. Very few would-be retirees seek advice, and it ends up hurting them badly.

The information below is meant solely as a primer to give you a leg up on what Social Security can do for you.

Social Security basics

The Social Security Act provides three types of benefits to qualified individuals:

- retirement
- disability
- survivor's benefits

The retirement benefit can be subdivided into direct payments to you and spousal benefits to your spouse, based on your work record. I'll get more into spousal benefits a bit later.

Social Security benefits begin the first day of the month following your chosen starting point. If a Social Security check is issued for the month of death, that check must be returned. Thus, participants don't receive a check for their first month of eligibility or the month that they die.

A few words on Social Security contributions

Employees and employers each pay 6.2 percent of covered wages into the system, up to each year's old-age, survivors, and disability insurance (OASDI) maximum earnings. The OASDI maximum earnings for 2013 is $113,700. Employees and employers also each pay 1.45 percent into the system each year for Medicare (there is no maximum for Medicare payments).

The Social Security base is computed over thirty-five years, and you need at least forty quarters to qualify for benefits. For purposes of our discussion, let's assume you retired in 2011 at age fifty-five and had maximum OASDI earnings for ten years from 2001 to 2010. You would have the equivalent of between $25,000 and $30,000 per year (remember, the base is an index), earned over thirty-five years. Because the Social Security system gives greatest weight to workers earning most of their dollars in the 90 and 32 percent levels, they get a lot of benefit from those last ten years. The idea here is, you want your highest paying years to go into the computation of your Social Security benefits, and for most of us, those years are at the end of our working life.

Note that *only* the employee portion counts for self-employed persons. Because they are also the employer, they may also pay the employer portion. The employer portion is *not* included in the Social Security benefit calculation. Note also that if self-employed persons have employees, they will be responsible for the employer portion of their employees' OASDI and Medicare payments.

Quarters for Social Security are earned on an annual basis. No more than four quarters may be earned in a single year. In 2013, a quarter of eligibility requires $1,160 of qualifying earnings. Thus, qualifying earnings over $4,640 earn four quarters of eligibility. Note that earning quarters each calendar year are based entirely upon qualifying earnings in that calendar year, not days, months, or quarters worked. As noted, you need to have a work record of at least forty quarters of qualifying earnings to receive Social Security benefits.

Let's dig a little deeper. If you've only earned a modest or low income over your thirty-five years of working, you'll feel better after you read the following. It gets a bit complicated, so bear with me. It'll be worth the slog.

Pointer: Social Security is not a true retirement plan, like a corporate or government pension that is typically weighed on the highest earnings at the end of a worker's career. Social Security benefits are based upon layering. In other words, they're indexed.

In 2013, the first $791.08 of average monthly earnings, or $9,492.96 for twelve months, accrues a monthly benefit (when retiring) at 90 percent credit. You are credited 90 percent of these amounts toward your Social Security benefits at full retirement age. That's pretty good if you don't earn much money. It means what dollars you do earn are earning a high credit toward your eventual benefits.

Between $791.08 and $4,768 average monthly earnings benefits are accrued at 32 percent (12 times for annual amount). Now you're getting less of the funds credited toward your Social Security benefits at full retirement age, but your calculations are based on a higher number, so you're better off than the guy who's getting 90 percent credit on a lower number, if that makes sense.

Average monthly earnings over $4,768 mean your benefits are accrued at 15 percent. That's fine, because it means you're a relatively high earner and will have a bigger pot of Social Security benefits when you reach full retirement age.

Pointer: Very low income earners get a much higher percentage of their wages subject to Social Security in eventual Social Security benefits.

Many advisers get confused

If you found the above explanation a bit confusing, you're in good company. Even tax, investment, and insurance professionals often misunderstand Social Security. Retirement pensions are typically based upon what is called "final pay." Final pay is typically an average of the last two, three, or five years of earnings. However, Social Security is based upon a "career average." The career average is based upon the best thirty-five years of Social Security earnings, indexed in the manner described above.

Look at it this way. Someone averaging roughly $25,000 per year in today's dollars earns over 2.5 times the annual 90 percent level per year in credit toward eventual Social Security benefits. Thus, in their first 14 (35/2.5) years of employment, they have earned the full 90 percent layer. Higher earners often go through both the 90 percent layer and the 32 percent layer by age fifty. The bottom line is that it almost never pays to try to boost Social Security benefits in the last five years of your career, unless you have a very short work history. The better strategy is to use the tax savings from the expenses by making a tax-deductible contribution into an SEP IRA, IRA, or 401(k).

What does the government say about my benefit level?

Those of you who are considering retirement should take a look at the Social Security website (www.ssa.gov). It's quite informative and will give you a great start on learning the basics before you even broach the topic of Social Security with your financial adviser, CPA, or tax attorney.

Here's a little more on how your contributions count, this time from the government's perspective. You'll see a bit of redundancy between the following quote and the above presentation about layering, but I think it's worth repeating a key concept like this. So here goes.

According to the website: "Social Security benefits are based on your lifetime earnings. Your actual earnings are adjusted or 'indexed' to account for changes in average wages since the year the earnings were received. Then Social Security calculates your average indexed monthly earnings during the 35 years in which you earned the most. We apply a formula to these earnings and arrive at your basic benefit, or 'primary insurance amount' (PIA). This is how much you would receive at your full retirement age—sixty-five or older, depending on your date of birth."

Pointer: Your best thirty-five years count. Your Social Security isn't calculated like a pension, which is a very good thing indeed!

A few words about government employees

You may or may not be aware of it, but some employees don't pay into Social Security. For example, a teacher's union can negotiate a retirement package based on a pension without the added Social Security component. The thinking is if the employer's 6.2 percent contribution for Social Security can be eliminated and instead folded into funding the pension or passed on to employees in the form of a slightly higher paycheck, everybody wins. The problem with that kind of arrangement is it knocks Social Security out of the picture, unless the employee takes steps to qualify for Social Security by working another job that pays into the program. Most of us do pay into Social Security, but for those of you who don't, the Social Security Administration says the following:

"If you also get or are eligible for a pension from work where you did not pay Social Security taxes (usually a government job), a different formula is applied to your average indexed monthly earnings."

The formula involves something called the Windfall Elimination Provisions (WEP), and it definitely influences your benefits. There is more information on the Social Security website. Check it out. For our purposes here, it's enough for me to point out that government employees who have not paid into Social Security must take special steps in order to qualify and earn benefits.

Actions that will reduce your benefits

Social Security wage earners can apply for Social Security benefits at age sixty-two. However, they will find their benefits reduced by several factors:

1. The early drawing reduction of 5/9 of 1 percent for every month prior to full retirement age of sixty-six if benefits begin thirty-six months (or fewer) prior to FRA. However, for an eligible person drawing more than thirty-six months early, the reduction is 5/12 of 1 percent for each month over thirty-six.

2. Excess earnings over the allowed earnings for that year reduce Social Security benefits by one-half the excess.

3. However, the Social Security benefits not currently received are not truly lost. The worker's benefits will be increased at FRA to account for benefits withheld due to earlier earnings.

I will get more into the issues surrounding taking benefits early or deferring them a little later.

Supplemental Social Security Income

Some people qualify for Supplemental Security Income (SSI) and have Medicaid pay their Social Security costs. Qualification for Supplemental Security Income is common for very low income individuals, disabled individuals, and special-needs individuals. Supplemental Security Income is a federal income supplement program designed to benefit the aged, blind, and disabled; benefits are used for food, clothing, and shelter.

Supplemental Security Income and Medicaid may pay Medicare costs for qualified individuals. However, Social Security qualification is required for Medicare. Thus, Medicaid can't pay for Medicare unless you qualify for Social Security. Qualification is very complex and beyond the scope of this book. I encourage families of potentially qualified individuals to contact someone with appropriate education and experience for assistance with these cases. Indeed, I frequently recommend hiring competent legal assistance to help prepare all Social Security disability applications. In fact, the Social Security Administration will subsidize the process after your application is denied twice.

Qualifying for Social Security disability income

Disability for Social Security purposes is for people who "cannot work because they have a medical condition that is expected to last at least one year, or result in death." Qualification for Social Security disability has been the subject of much debate and criticism for years. Until recently, "disability" was defined as permanent and total disability. The current definition makes it easier to qualify and exposes the entire Social Security system to increased costs. Nevertheless, the qualification process frequently involves multiple applications and reapplications.

Denial of Social Security disability claims is so common and the application process is so cumbersome that many people choose to hire specialized attorneys to help apply (or reapply after denial). After claims have been denied twice, the government may even help pay these attorneys. "Current qualification" for Social Security Disability Income (SSDI) requires a consistent work history. To be qualified for Social Security requires the following:

a. Before age twenty-four, a worker must have six quarters of coverage or half the quarters since age twenty-one.

b. Between age twenty-four and age thirty, a worker needs credit for half the quarters after age twenty-one.

c. After age thirty-one, a worker needs credit for twenty of the most recent forty quarters at the time of the disability onset.

Social Security disability benefits entitle beneficiaries to Medicare coverage after being entitled to benefits for twenty-four months (42 U.S.C. Section 426(b)(2): 42 CFR, Section 406.12). However, after being entitled to Social Security disability benefits, you must wait a minimum of five months before Social Security benefits are payable.

To recap: Social Security disability benefits entitle the recipient to Medicare benefits as early as twenty-nine months after the Social Security disability application. Social Security disability may qualify a recipient for Medicare at any age after a five-month waiting period plus twenty-four months of disability. The twenty-four months need not be consecutive. Once Social Security disability recipients become eligible to receive regular Social Security, they are switched to regular Social Security.

Social Security benefits

Survivor benefits: When a spouse dies, the total benefits to the surviving spouse normally are the greater of the deceased spouse's benefits or the surviving spouse's own benefits. Surviving spouses do not get the benefits of both; they get the greater of their own benefits or their deceased spouse's benefits. Survivor benefits are a valuable part of Social Security.

To collect these benefits, you have to be legally married, and the spouse whose benefits are drawn upon has to have qualified to receive benefits. Couples married for only nine months qualify as surviving spouses. However, to receive full survivor spousal benefits, you must have reached FRA.

There may be a reduced survivor benefit if the deceased spouse had remarried and was either married at time of death (nine months for surviving spouses to qualify) or had been married more than once for at least ten years. Survivor benefits are also reduced if either the deceased spouse started their benefits early *or* the surviving spouse draws survivor benefits before their own FRA. Survivor benefits can be affected by the existence of more than one qualifying spouse.

Pointer: The key is the surviving spouse's age. If the surviving spouse has reached FRA, they will generally receive full benefits. If the surviving spouse has not reached FRA, they will receive a reduced benefit unless they wait until FRA to receive survivor's benefits. Deferred benefits will exceed the nondeferred benefits. Remember, the surviving spouse is entitled to the greater of their benefit or benefits based upon the deceased spouse. Again, to get full benefits a surviving spouse must have reached full retirement age.

Spousal benefits: At full retirement age—sixty-six for persons born between 1943 and 1954—a participant can draw spousal benefits of 50 percent based upon the spouse's Social Security record while deferring and growing their own benefits at 8 percent per year between the age of sixty-six and the maximum of age seventy. Thus, at age sixty-six, you could draw half of your spouse's benefits and increase your own benefit by 32 percent until you reached the maximum at age seventy. At that point, you'd begin collecting your greatly increased benefits.

Using spousal benefits to enable the other spouse to defer taking Social Security benefits, thereby increasing the value of those benefits, represents an opportunity so poorly understood that it is estimated that fewer than 10 percent of Social Security participants choose the option. However, the benefit is awesome. The benefit also works for the spouse. If you were to die prematurely but after age seventy, your spouse could draw half of your now enhanced benefit of 132 percent of your age sixty-six benefit. The actual increase is 2/3 of 1 percent per month. At age sixty-seven, you would have a benefit of 108 percent of your age sixty-six benefit simply by deferring and taking advantage of spousal benefits. In the event of your death, your spouse would do better by 8 percent, provided that your spouse's Social Security benefits were less than yours. If they were greater, then your spouse would naturally take those instead.

Pointer: When there is an age difference of a few years, and the earnings records are similar, it will generally be best for the older member to begin receiving benefits at FRA and the younger to defer receiving retirement benefits at FRA. The younger member should elect to begin spousal benefits at FRA.

To illustrate:

Martin and Linda both have nearly maximum Social Security earnings records. However, there were subtle differences. Linda will reach her full retirement age in a few months. Martin is eighteen months younger. My initial thoughts were to advise Martin to continue employment and for Linda to defer her Social Security benefits. If Linda defers her benefits, they will not receive any Social Security for eighteen months. When Martin reaches FRA, he would like to retire. They will lose his current income of $10,000 per month.

If Linda begins her benefits now, they will have her full Social Security benefits for eighteen months, and when Martin reaches sixty-six, they will have Linda's full benefits plus Martin's spousal benefits when he reaches FRA from Martin's age sixty-six to age seventy. Linda begins drawing approximately $2,500 per month (the maximum for workers reaching FRA in 2012 is $2,513). Martin's spousal benefit beginning in eighteen months is approximately $1,250, and when Martin reaches age seventy, his enhanced benefit should be approximately $3,300 per month (132 percent of $2,500).

I'll get more into spousal benefits and the advantage of deferring Social Security in chapter 7. I did want to give you the basics here, though; you can't fully understand the enormous value of spousal benefits without putting them into the context of deferring one spouse's Social Security benefits.

Divorced spouses: Divorced ex-spouses may draw spousal benefits if they were married at least ten years and the ex-spouse is eligible to draw. Note that the law does not require the ex-spouse to be drawing. By contrast, it does require a current spouse to have applied for Social Security. This seems a reasonable provision to prevent ex-spouses from delaying drawing to hinder the availability of ex-spouse benefits. The rules for qualifying ex-spouses are also poorly understood. Spousal benefits and survivor benefits are automatic and do not require the approval of the ex-spouse (they may not even require the knowledge of the ex-spouse).

Divorced ex-spouse status requires ten years of marriage, versus almost immediate qualification as a current spouse. Remarriage terminates divorced ex-spouse status. If the second marriage ends as a result of death, divorce, or annulment in fewer than ten years, eligibility based on the first spouse can be reinstated. Ex-spouse benefits terminate upon remarriage.

A critical exception to the remarriage rules exists if the surviving divorced ex-spouse remarries after age sixty (or after age fifty if the surviving ex-spouse remarries after age fifty and is entitled to disability benefits at the time of the disability). In those cases, the Social Security rules disregard the remarriage.

To recap, qualification as a divorced ex-spouse on a former spouse's record requires that he or she

- was married to the ex-spouse for at least ten years,
- is at least sixty-two years old,
- is unmarried, and
- is not entitled to a higher Social Security benefit on his or her own record.

When qualified as an ex-spouse, taxpayers can choose to defer their own benefits and draw spousal benefits. It is not necessary that the ex-spouse begin drawing benefits, only that they have reached age sixty-two. This prevents ex-spouses from deferring their own Social Security qualification to spite their ex-spouse. In some cases, the only thing a qualifying ex-spouse needs to begin drawing spousal benefits is their ex-spouse's Social Security number and date of birth. Spousal benefits will rarely be affected by multiple ex-spouses, but survivor benefits are frequently limited.

When one member of a divorced couple dies, the total benefits go to the surviving spouse—normally the greater of the deceased spouse's benefits or the surviving spouse's own benefits. The surviving spouse does not get the benefit of both. They do, as explained earlier, get the greater of their own benefits or their deceased ex-spouse's benefits.

Pointer: Divorce may not only terminate spousal benefits but also eliminate eligibility for no cost Medicare Part A.

To illustrate:

Sherrie was married twice, but each time she was married for less than ten years. She has been a caregiver for her parents and in recent years for her brother. Thus, she has never accumulated enough credits (forty quarters or ten years) to qualify for Social Security benefits. Unfortunately, Sherrie is not in a relationship that qualifies her for Medicare.

She can purchase Medicare Part A hospitalization benefits, but the cost is very high. If she does not have thirty quarters of SS qualification, it will cost over $450 per month for Part A Medicare. Part A Medicare is free for all qualified Social Security participants and those who are qualifying ex-spouses or current spouses.

Note that if Sherrie had been married ten years, she would receive both spousal Social Security benefits and free Medicare Part A hospitalization.

Family benefits: The most valuable family benefit occurs when a Social Security participant has children under age eighteen. The Social Security participant must apply for Social Security to let their children draw. If the participant's spouse doesn't work, they may also draw benefits based upon the participant's Social Security record. Even though the participant must apply for Social Security, they may actually suspend their own benefits if the participant is of full retirement age, while enabling their spouse and children to receive benefits. Suspending the participant's benefits is particularly important if he or she is still working. Benefits grow and contributions to Social Security continue. These strategies are another poorly understood and therefore underutilized means of getting the most from Social Security benefits.

I recently gave a seminar to an audience of financial planners and certified public accountants; two CPAs had a question about a friend who was forty-nine and had just given birth to twins. Their friend's husband was sixty-three and retired. The spouse and children could draw well over $1,000 per month, but no one in the audience was aware of the opportunity.

Pointer: Family benefit limits vary, but they generally equal or exceed 150 percent of the worker's benefits. The limit on family benefits allowable on one's Social Security record may limit both a current spouse's survivor benefits and the former spouse's survivor benefits. It is, however, unlikely that spousal benefits will be limited.

Family members who may receive benefits include the following:

- the worker
- the worker's spouse (married to the worker for at least one year immediately preceding the application for spouse's benefits)

- the worker's qualifying divorced spouse (married ten years)
- the worker's surviving spouse (married nine months immediately prior to death)
- the worker's surviving divorced spouse
- the worker's child (under eighteen or full-time elementary or secondary student under nineteen or disabled before age twenty-two)
- the worker's parent

Pointer: When a worker's spouse is caring for their young child under age sixteen, the spouse is entitled to Social Security benefits if the worker is qualified and applied for Social Security, the worker is disabled, or the worker is deceased.

Therefore, it may be very important for the worker to begin Social Security benefits. This can entitle the spouse to receive benefits based upon caring for the child (or children) under age sixteen and the children eighteen and under or age nineteen and still a full-time elementary or secondary student.

The requirements to be "a spouse of a retired worker" are met by meeting any of the following conditions:

a. Have a child under age sixteen or a qualifying disabled child of any age under his or her care.

b. Qualifying as a current spouse and being at least sixty-two years old. Note: spousal benefits do not require qualifying children. They do require that the worker has applied for Social Security benefits or that the spouse be age sixty-two or greater.

c. Qualifying as a divorced ex-spouse. This condition is met if they were married ten years and the spouse did not remarry (the worker may have remarried).

Pointer: Drawing benefits as a spouse caring for a retired or deceased participant's child does not reduce future spousal or survivor benefits.

A few words on taxes

Spousal benefits are part of the Social Security taxability determination for the parent's joint return. If the family's modified adjusted gross income (MAGI) exceeds $32,000 for Married Filing Joint status, the benefits will be directly taxable. Children's Social Security benefits are seldom taxable (if the $32,000 modified adjusted gross income standard is exceeded) because children seldom have $25,000 of modified adjusted gross income.

Current tax rules for Social Security benefits begin taxation at $25,000 of modified adjusted gross income for single taxpayers and $32,000 for married taxpayers. One-half of Social Security benefits are includible in the MAGI calculation.

Parting words: As I said at the outset, very few laypeople (and surprisingly few financial advisers) have a real handle on the complicated fine print of Social Security. It behooves you to find an adviser who knows this stuff inside and out. In its current form, Social Security is a powerful tool that can help you achieve your retirement dreams.

7

Early Birds Don't Get the Worm

IN TODAY'S TOUGH ECONOMIC times, it's not surprising that a large number of people opt to take their Social Security early. I understand why you might do that. If you retired early, you may need the money to pay your bills. Or you may need the early Social Security benefits to enable you to retire early. But if you look at the big picture, myriad reasons emerge that should tell you in no uncertain terms that taking Social Security early carries a basket of potential financial liabilities for you and your spouse.

As I've already mentioned, benefits are reduced 5/9 of 1 percent for each month prior to when full retirement age (FRA) benefits would begin. However, for an eligible person drawing more than thirty-six months prior to FRA, the reduction is 5/9 of 1 percent each month for the first thirty-six months and 5/12 of 1 percent for each month over thirty-six. That's a lot of cash you missed out on because you were anxious to grab the bucks and hit the golf course.

There's more. If you defer taking your Social Security between age sixty-six and age seventy, you'll see your benefits increased to 2/3 of 1 percent for every month of deferral after full retirement age up to age seventy, or an increase in your benefit equal to 8 percent per year. That's even more of an incentive to wait. In the past, some would say that taking the benefits early was okay because you could invest the money and generate a hefty return, well in excess of 8 percent. The current low interest environment and poor stock market performance since 2000 makes drawing benefits early and investing the money less desirable than at any time during the last thirty years. Conversely, the combination of poor investment opportunities and increased benefits from deferring Social Security benefits after FRA make increasing retirement benefits through deferral much more attractive than at any time in the past.

Remember the spousal benefit from the last chapter? That's the one where you can draw half of your spouse's age sixty-six Social Security benefit from your full retirement age up to age seventy. If your spouse is drawing Social Security benefits on his or her own work record, the deferring spouse can also draw spousal benefits during the period of deferral of up to 50 percent. Since the deferred benefits have a greater lifetime expectancy than the value of drawing beginning at full retirement age, the spousal benefits become a huge bonus to the deferring spouse. In other words, play the Social Security game right, and you come out a real winner. Play it wrong, and you lose big.

Pointer: Here's a recap of what it costs to take your Social Security early:

- More than three years early (sixty-two to sixty-three): 5/12 of 1 percent per month.
- The three years prior to full retirement age (sixty-three to sixty-six): 5/9 of 1 percent per month.
- After full retirement age (sixty-six), there is an increase of 2/3 of 1 percent for each month of deferral.

Drawing Social Security at age sixty-two causes retirees born between 1943 and 1954 to lose 25 percent per year of potential Social Security benefits for life versus waiting until full retirement age. The table below further illustrates my point:

Social Security Benefit for Retirees Born between 1943 and 1954 Assume Age 66 Benefits Are $2,000 per Month			
Begin Benefits At:	**One Year Adds**	**Total Addition**	Total Annual Income Gain
62 $1,500			
63 $1,600	6.7%	$100	
64 $1,733	8.3%	$233	
65 $1,867	7.7%	$367	
66 $2,000	7.1%	$500	
67 $2,160	8.0%	$660	
68 $2,333	8.0%	$833	
69 $2,519	8.0%	$1,019	
70 $2,721	8.0%	$1,221	81%

Theories about the appropriate time to begin Social Security benefits have changed dramatically over the last twenty-five years. Here are the primary reasons:

1. Earning rates on short-term bank deposits have declined over 90 percent.

2. Stock market results during the two decades from 1980 to 2000 averaged well over 15 percent per year.

3. Since 2000, the average annual return for the S&P 500 Index has been less than 1 percent per year.

4. Life expectancies have increased.

5. Social Security benefits from deferring benefits between full retirement age and age seventy have been dramatically increased.

6. Survivor benefits influence more retirees because more retirees have a living spouse.

A few words on life expectancy

Not convinced about deferral yet? Okay, then. Let's dig into this subject a bit more.

First, if you are married, don't just look at individual life expectancy when you're doing your retirement planning. You need to look at joint life expectancy, because it has a direct bearing on what you're going to do when it comes time to decide whether you want to defer full Social Security benefits for one spouse or not. Joint life expectancy is defined as the 50 percent likelihood that one member of the couple will be living at the life expectancy. For example, if the life expectancy of two seventy-year-old spouses is twenty-five years, it means there is a 50 percent chance one of them will live until age ninety-five.

If the higher-earning spouse defers receiving their Social Security benefits until age seventy, the likelihood is that one or both will receive the increased benefits for a combined life expectancy, possibly for as many as thirty years. In other words, if you both live into your early nineties, the additional ten to fifteen years you each live add up to twenty years or more, meaning you collected increased benefits for that long.

Pointer: Principles of Social Security provide benefits to the survivor of their own benefits, or their spouse's benefit, whichever is higher. Thus, ideally the higher earner defers receiving their benefits until age seventy. Factors of health and relative age must also be considered.

As I've said, retirees today can expect to live a much longer period after retiring. When Social Security initially started providing seniors cash flow, the remaining life expectancy was less than five years. Thus, Social Security was a benefit many people didn't live to enjoy, and if they reached Social Security qualification, they weren't expected to receive benefits long before they died. Government projections did not anticipate the length of current retirements or the number of people living to enjoy retirement. That's a major problem for younger boomers, and that's why you may very well see the game changed. The change will not be in your favor.

Pointer: If you can afford to do so and are healthy, deferring Social Security benefits makes perfect sense. On the other hand, if you really need the money, and you or your spouse are in poor health, then taking early benefits or benefits at full retirement age isn't necessarily a huge mistake. Reducing benefits due to early receipt of Social Security reduces your family's assets, so consider purchasing life insurance or an annuity with increasing death benefits to protect your family.

To illustrate:

Two of my clients, Andy and Lisa, faced some complicated planning decisions related to deferring Social Security benefits. I suggested that Andy defer drawing his Social Security until age seventy. The extra $700 per month Social Security projected at age seventy seemed critical to their retirement quality.

Andy and Lisa quickly embraced this suggestion. Lisa asked about the risk that Andy might not live long enough to make up the difference. She calculated $25,200 per year foregone Social Security for each of four years. The $100,800 total seemed hard to replicate. She wondered how they could be sure that the benefit of $700 per month more cash flow starting when Andy reached age seventy would exceed the lost benefits of $100,800. I answered that there was no guarantee that it would, but that the odds overwhelmingly favored this strategy.

I detailed the following information:

1. Break-even time based upon Andy's life alone was twelve years ($100,800/$700 = 144 months or twelve years).

2. Lisa's survivor benefit essentially means if either of them lived more than twelve years, they would be ahead.

3. Insurance industry averages show the combined life expectancy for a seventy-year-old couple is approximately twenty-five years.

4. Andy may draw spousal benefits of $900 plus per month for the four years between his age sixty-six and age seventy. The monthly "give-up" for Andy will be not $2,100 per month but only $1,200 per month. Therefore, the break-even time for Andy and Lisa should be calculated based upon forty-eight months of losing $1,200 per month. Losing $57,600 will be made up in eighty-three months. Andy was ecstatic. He realized that when he was seventy-seven (his age seventy, plus seven years), they would be ahead for the rest of time either of them lived.

Deferral concept makes sense even if you're not rich

You might think that you have to be rich to defer taking Social Security to maximize the collective benefits you and your spouse are eligible for, but that's not always the case. In fact, most people just don't think before they make decisions about their Social Security benefits. If they did, then they'd see that their best interests would be served if they took the big picture into account. This is even more important if you're working with a low retirement income and few assets.

One client I advised was a very prominent university math professor. He researched Social Security, but none of the sources he viewed suggested maximizing a couple's benefits. He expressed concern that the only break-even point he found on the Social Security website was for an individual. However, given the number of married seniors and formerly married seniors, the joint life expectancy deserves more attention. I believe for couples it is the only relevant consideration for their combined benefit.

The opportunity for one spouse to defer and dramatically increase their benefits while drawing spousal benefits is little known and seldom used. Unfortunately, many people do not read, seek counsel, or interview Social Security personnel prior to choosing their retirement strategy. The most common approach is simply to get as much as you can as soon as you can. If you do this, then chances are you're shooting yourself in the foot.

To illustrate:

Assume Sam is sixty-six, with projected SS benefits of $1,200 per month. Sally, his sixty-four-year-old wife, has $800 per month in benefits based on her record. If Sally begins to draw her benefits, Sam can draw spousal benefits based upon her benefits at FRA of sixty-six. Sam would get 50 percent of Sally's projected age sixty-six benefits of $960. Thus, Sam and Sally would have total SS benefits of $800 from Sally and $480 from Sam's half of Sally's benefits. Their current monthly cash flow loss is $2,000 less $1,280, or $720. Sam should seek part-time work to produce at least $720 per month to meet their expected $2,000 per month cash flow requirements.

If Sam defers from age sixty-six to age seventy, it will increase the family cash flow $400 per month as long as either of them lives. In early 2013, Merrill Lynch adjusted their estimate of the acceptable rate of retirement distributions to 3.5 percent. Thus, it takes $137,142.85 of extra assets at 3.5 percent to earn $400 per month more Social Security income. Sam and Sally don't have much more than that in their IRAs and in the form of other assets. They are like many couples today, who rely on Social Security as the main instrument for cash flow during retirement. It makes sense, then, that they'd want to do everything possible to increase that cash flow through sound planning and financial management.

As previously mentioned, it's unfortunate that most advisers know little or nothing about the spousal benefit aspects of Social Security, and that retirees generally aren't told about the many benefits of deferring Social Security, but that's the way it is nowadays. With deferring Social Security in mind, I caution against early retirement and not working part-time during your retirement. The cash flow shortfalls from deferring need to be made up somewhere. It's the big picture that should drive your retirement strategy, not short-term gratification.

The long view of breaking even

When discussions about deferring Social Security come up, inevitably someone talks about the "break-even" point. Unfortunately, every calculation I have seen emphasizes the break-even point based upon individuals, when the total package, both your and your spouse's Social Security benefits, should be the key determining factor behind your joint decisions for retirement. If you're single, the calculation for breaking even, the point at which your increased benefits gained by deferral pay for the amount you received by taking Social Security early, become a little less salient. Again, it's when you're planning and managing retirement as a couple that the value of strategic planning fully comes to bear.

To illustrate:

Let's take a look at a couple earning between $50,000 and $60,000.

Harold is within six months of his full retirement age of sixty-six. He received projections showing an expected benefit at sixty-six of $1,500 per month. If he defers receiving benefits until age seventy, his benefit will be approximately $2,000 per month. His CPA did the following analysis for him:

Lost benefits for forty-eight months of $1,500 per month = $72,000

Incremental benefits = $500 per month ($2,000 less $1,500)

Conclusion: break-even time is 144 months, or twelve years

The break-even period for deferring retirement benefits until age seventy will be substantially less for single persons if they have previously been married for more than ten years to a Social Security wage earner with a good earning record. The combination of the Social Security benefits drawn as a qualifying ex-spouse (between their own age sixty-six and age seventy) and the dramatically higher benefits their own record pays after age seventy make this decision a very important step in preparing for retirement.

An about-face may be possible

As of January 1, 2011, during the first twelve months of receiving Social Security benefits, the taxpayer may repay the amount received *without* interest. This allows taxpayers the option of choosing a new plan that may better suit their future needs. Only one withdrawal from Social Security is allowed per lifetime. This one-year limit superseded the earlier ruling allowing Social Security benefits to be repaid any time until age seventy.

To illustrate:

Frank was able repay his Social Security benefits of $2,200 per month without interest just prior to the one-year (twelve-month) deadline. Frank's current plan is to defer drawing his Social Security benefits until he reaches age seventy. We expect Frank's Social Security beginning in late 2016, when he turns seventy, to be approximately $3,400 per month. Sally's survivor benefits, should Frank die first, will be the higher of either her Social Security or Frank's, in this case the $3,400.

Once Frank reaches full retirement age of sixty-six, he will be able to draw spousal benefits based upon Sally's Social Security benefits record. Sally must be drawing her own Social Security benefits in order to allow Frank to receive spousal benefits.

A few words on work

Workers with substantially fewer than thirty-five good earning years for Social Security will get a greater increase in their Social Security benefits by continuing to work even after they are eligible to begin drawing benefits. These workers will substitute good earning years for years with either no earnings or very little earnings. Workers with nearly thirty-five years of maximum earnings will gain almost nothing by continuing to work.

If you work after you start collecting Social Security benefits but before your FRA and exceed the established earning limit (about $15,000 for 2014), part or all of your benefits will be suspended. The lost benefits are added to future benefits. Thus, they are not lost but merely deferred. Family benefits remain in effect when a worker has applied for Social Security benefits but earns too much to receive benefits. Thus, many people should apply at age sixty-two, even if they expect to earn too much, depending on their need for family benefits.

Parting words: You must weigh many factors when deciding at which point you and your spouse decide to collect Social Security benefits of any kind. As you can see, the program is more complicated and more comprehensive than you probably imagined. For many of us, Social Security was all about a direct monthly payment from Uncle Sam to you, and then a survivor benefit for your spouse if you were married for more than ten years. You probably also were aware of Social Security disability benefits. But now you can see that the program offers much more, and that the timing of benefit collection can play a critical role in bolstering or weakening your cash flow during retirement. What might seem to be an obvious course of action often is the wrong way to go.

Study the information in this book, get on the Social Security Administration website, and consult with an adviser who knows enough about Social Security to offer you sound advice. The big shortfall in most traditional financial advisers is that they are salespeople first. Broader issues impacting you as a senior or soon-to-be senior don't fall within the scope of expertise required to sell financial products. That's why you should be assisted by someone with the breadth of knowledge on Social Security, Medicare, annuities, alternative investments, traditional investment vehicles, and taxes. Chances are you're going to need several advisers, as I indicated earlier. With the right advice, you can harness the incredible power of your Social Security dollars to get you on your way to a quality retirement.

8

Medicare and You

BACK IN 1965, CONGRESS passed Title XVIII of the Social Security Act to make health care insurance available to Americans over the age of sixty-five, and to make it available for certain groups of younger people under specified conditions. It was a grand plan designed to combat the expenses of medical coverage that were rising even back then, and in the intervening years, Medicare has become a hugely popular entitlement program. Taken together with its older but still closely related sister, Social Security, both programs form the backbone of the safety net for you as a retiree. However, the system is complicated and has many potentially lethal financial landmines you've got to avoid, and to do that requires a good working knowledge of the program's advantages and pitfalls.

As with Social Security, big changes are just over the horizon. As Congress and the executive branch work toward lowering the budget deficit and our national debt, millions of baby boomers are going to reach retirement age. The combined impact of cuts to Social Security and Medicare in conjunction with the influx of retirees that are dependent upon both is bound to create trouble for individuals of modest or lower means. It also may require wealthier individuals to pay more and possibly get less. The good news is that sound financial planning now can mitigate the damage any drastic future changes to both programs might do to you on an individual basis if you are a younger boomer. If you're already at or near the age of full retirement, then you'll see no major changes that will directly impact your life. It's a totally different story for your kids and grandkids, and it's one you should keep in mind as an actively involved American citizen.

So what is Medicare all about? Let's start off with a really superficial summary. I'll go into much more detail later in this chapter. The objective is to give you a good idea of what makes the program tick and how to choose the maximum coverage at the least expense to you as a retiree. Don't be tempted to cut corners. Dealing with and paying for health problems affects every retiree. Even if you live in perfect health until you die, chances are someone close to you, possibly your spouse, won't be as lucky.

Medicare 101

The four key parts of the program are comprised of Part A, Part B, Part C, and Part D.

- Part A covers hospital services.
- Part B covers doctor services.
- Part C covers Medicare Advantage plans.
- Part D covers prescription drugs.

Most preexisting conditions don't boot you from Medicare

Everyone meeting the eligibility rules qualifies for Medicare Parts A, B, C, and D in the first six months of Medicare eligibility, beginning the month in which the individual reaches age sixty-five. Eligibility typically also accrues when coverage is established within sixty-three days of losing or ending certain types of coverage, including private health insurance supplements to Medicare coverage. There is no exclusion for preexisting conditions for Medicare Parts A, B, or D if implemented within three months of reaching age sixty-five or losing equivalent employer coverage, whichever is later (however, there is an exclusion for end-stage renal failure). No one is required to pay higher premiums because of existing medical conditions.

Medicare Part A

Medicare Part A is hospital insurance for hospital expenses, and it's free if you have a work record of forty or more quarters with Social Security (more on eligibility and other potential costs later). Part A pays inpatient care in hospitals for the first sixty days of hospitalization (subject to a $1,100 deductible), skilled nursing facilities, hospice, and home health care.

Hospital services under Medicare Part A include the following:

- Care in a semiprivate room, meals, general nursing, and other hospital services and supplies.
- Care in a critical access hospital.
- Inpatient mental health care. For days one through sixty, there is an initial deductible (the patient pays the first $1,156).
- For days sixty-one through ninety, the patient pays an additional $289 per day.
- After day ninety, the patient has a lifetime reserve of $578 per day for sixty additional days.

For days one through ninety, the deductibles are per qualifying hospital stay (a qualified stay occurs when the patient is in the hospital officially as an in-patient, generally more than twenty-three hours). Once patients have gone sixty days between stays, they can start a new hospital stay. The lifetime reserve is one per lifetime. Once the lifetime reserve is used, there is no Medicare coverage for stays beyond ninety days. Medicare enrollees are fully responsible for medical costs once the Medicare eligibility time frame per hospital stay is exceeded. Even if the family is able to negotiate a reduced rate, once eligibility is exhausted, the risk of exhausting the personal resources of the Medicare enrollee is very substantial.

Medicare enrollees and their families should be very aware of the time between hospital stays. If at least sixty days pass between hospital stays, the second stay is considered a new hospital stay as opposed to an extension of the previous hospital stay. Failing to obtain coverage for the large costs of extended hospital stays is a critical mistake made time after time by seniors and their advisers when planning for and managing retirement expenses. Medicare supplement plans, which I'll discuss in detail, substantially reduce this risk. Another common senior mistake is failure to protect themselves against long-term care expenses, which I'll get to in chapter 11.

Medicare Advantage plans under Medicare Part C typically do little or nothing to resolve the problems of low-cost hospital coverage being limited to sixty days and high co-pays between day sixty-one and day ninety. The cost goes even higher for those forced to use the sixty-day lifetime reserve for hospital stays over ninety days. Medicare Advantage plans will be discussed at length later in this chapter.

Pointer: Individual and business health care insurance policies typically establish a dollar limit on benefits but not a time limit. Some people call these limits "Major Medical" (an outdated term). Medicare Part A (hospital coverage) and Medicare Advantage plans do not have a dollar limit for benefits, but there is both a reduced payment limit beginning at day sixty-one for each hospital stay and a time limit for extended hospital stays. Keep this important distinction in mind when you start thinking about balancing costs with coverage.

Medicare Part B

Although Medicare Part A is generally free, an eligible participant must enroll in and pay for Medicare Part B to receive Medicare Part A coverage. You cannot purchase Medicare Part B unless you either qualified to receive Medicare Part A for free or you bought Medicare

Part A. Coverage under Parts A and B are required for coverage under Parts C (Medicare Advantage plans) and D (drug plans). Confused yet? No worries. It'll all become clear in a little while. The point is, you're already seeing how each piece of the program is linked to the other in some way. Believe me, it gets better!

What you get in Medicare Part B

Medicare Part B pays eligible, medically necessary services including doctors' services, outpatient care, and home health services. Durable medical equipment costs are also covered. Under Medicare Part B, patients must pay 20 percent of these costs under coinsurance provisions. Some preventive services are covered.

There is a cost for Part B coverage that is standard for individuals with under $85,000 adjusted gross income (AGI) and for couples with under $170,000 AGI. The general rule is that Medicare premiums are based upon your AGI on the last tax return available from the IRS. Because Medicare premiums reset January 1 of each year, that will generally be the return for TWO years previous.

Medicare will review cases where income drops or marital status changes. For information on Medicare appeals due to changed circumstances, see SSA Publication No. 05-10536. When income has dropped substantially in the last two years or new marital status would reduce Medicare premiums, participants should appeal to Medicare for premium reduction. Individuals still working and receiving employer health insurance deemed to be as good as Medicare benefits will not be penalized if they enroll on a timely basis after ending employer coverage. The employer should provide an annual statement that the worker is covered by a plan equivalent or better than Medicare.

Pointer: You can opt out of Medicare Part B in the initial seven-month Medicare enrollment period, but you could face a 10 percent per year cost increase in the coverage for every year you weren't signed up for Part B if you go for coverage later.

A few words on Social Security and qualifying for Medicare

Eligibility for free full Medicare coverage under Part A requires that a worker have a Social Security record of forty or more quarters. Eligibility may be earned based upon your own Social Security record or qualification as a spouse of a qualifying worker, a spouse of a deceased worker, or as a divorced ex-spouse of a worker. In rare cases, qualification may be received by being a surviving parent of a qualified Social Security participant.

Workers without eligibility for Social Security should strive to become eligible, as it is critical in establishing Medicare eligibility. Persons with less than forty quarters of Social Security eligibility should earn more quarters by working enough to earn four quarters each year if they cannot qualify for Medicare coverage as a spouse or divorced ex-spouse of a qualifying worker. Partial Social Security coverage (but not enough for eligibility) reduces the cost of Medicare Part A for individuals with less than forty quarters of credit with Social Security.

In 2012, individuals with thirty to thirty-nine quarters of Social Security coverage paid $248 per month for Medicare Part A coverage. That represented a savings of $203 per month versus individuals with up to twenty-nine quarters of coverage, who had to pay a premium of $451 per month. Earning as little as $4,520 in 2012 could have earned you four quarters of Social Security coverage, thereby saving you $2,412, plus inflation, annually in Medicare costs. Buying Part A will protect yourself from full exposure to hospitalization bills if you haven't fully met Part A eligibility requirements.

Pointer: Before you apply for Medicare, make sure you have forty quarters of Social Security in your own work record (or that you can qualify as specified above). If need be, keep working to earn Social Security credit to help offset what you'll pay toward Medicare Part A. Remember, you can't get Part B without having Part A.

Low income retirees: Persons receiving very small Social Security checks will receive free Medicare Part A, which is worth $451 per month. Medicare eligible participants with limited income should contact their local Social Security Administration office to inquire about programs that may offer help with health care needs covered under Medicare Part B and Part D. The extra help programs may pay 100 percent of prescription costs. These limited or no income persons frequently qualify for enriched benefits provided by a combination of Medicare and Medicaid. These enriched benefits are often called a "shared plan." At present, this is something of a safety net for seniors with very low income.

Medicare Part C

Medicare Part C is now known under the catchall name of Medicare Advantage plans. The old name for Part C was simply Medicare + Choice. Both names try to get at the basic premise that as long as you have Medicare Parts A and B, you can get a Medicare Advantage plan that will allow you to receive your health care through a provider organization like a health maintenance organization (HMO) or a preferred provider organization (PPO). The idea is that certain plans will lower costs, and the plans can increase benefits or an additional monthly premium. For example, about 70 percent of the available Medicare Advantage plans almost replace Part D for drug coverage. There are advantages and disadvantages to Medicare Advantage plans. Careful consideration should be given before making any decisions.

Medicare Part D

Medicare Part D drug coverage resulted from the Medicare Prescription Drug, Improvement, and Modernization Act of 2003. Part D coverage became available in 2006. Coverage is available only through insurance companies and HMOs. Part D coverage may be purchased in the initial Medicare eligibility period by anyone covered under Parts A and B.

Alternatively, some people choose to get Medicare Parts A and B through a private insurer under a Medicare Advantage plan. I'll tell you more about these plans in a minute. Suffice it to say here that Medicare Advantage plans may offer Part D drug coverage free or require enrollees to pay for the coverage. However, it is important to note that Medicare Advantage plan members are not allowed by Medicare authorities to have separate Part D coverage. The reason separate Part D coverage is not allowed is to keep seniors from mistakenly buying duplicate coverage, since coverage is included in Medicare Advantage plans.

Medicare Part D coverage is voluntary. You have to opt in if you want it when you sign up for Medicare. There is a relatively small cost per month, totaling approximately $500 per year. There are co-pays that vary, depending on the cost category of the drug.

To illustrate:

Let's say that Part D coverage costs $42.10 per month. The $505.20 annual cost may save $320 on the first prescription costs, leaving only $185.20 of potential costs for even the healthiest Medicare participants. Thus, even a Medicare enrollee with between $25 and $30 per month prescription costs would only have a potential cost of approximately $185 per year if the Part D coverage covers the basic deductible. I believe virtually all Medicare enrollees should have prescription coverage. If a participant feels they can't afford even $42.10 per month, they should consider a Medicare Advantage plan that includes Part D coverage with no cost.

Another hitch or two

There is a 10 percent per year surcharge for years where no Part D coverage is elected by the taxpayer. A taxpayer who does not choose Part D coverage until age seventy-two would pay a monthly premium of 170 percent more than the amount paid by a comparably aged person who chose coverage at age sixty-five and continued the coverage every year. Seniors who live a normal or longer life expectancy will generally rue the decision not to start Part D coverage when first eligible. For clients with an attained age of sixty-five to seventy, I generally estimate life expectancy at eighty for men and eighty-five for women. When clients are already over seventy, I add half a year for every year over seventy. Eligibility generally begins with age sixty-five.

Pointer: Workers employed and covered by their employer's health insurance plans may delay the start of eligibility for Part D without the 10 percent per year surcharge.

A few words on the infamous doughnut hole

At present, Medicare Part D standard costs are structured in such a way that some retirees find they fall into a gap where coverage gets turned off. The shrieks from those who find themselves in this position reverberate throughout the country, and for good reason. Prescription drugs are expensive, especially if you take a lot of them. Medicare Advantage plans frequently pay part of the costs below, which is better than having no help at all.

Here are the standard costs for Medicare Part D coverage in 2012:

Stage 1. Participant pays $320 deductible.

Stage 2. Between $320 and $2,930, the plan pays 75 percent and the participant pays 25 percent.

Stage 3. Between $2,930 and $4,700, the participant pays the full cost. This is called the doughnut hole. Yikes! You can imagine how much this could hurt if you are of limited means.

Stage 4. Over $4,700, the plan pays 75 percent and the participant pays 25 percent.

About your prescription drugs

Prescription drugs are grouped into five tiers. Each tier becomes progressively more expensive for the Medicare enrollee. The tiers are:

Tier 1 (preferred generic): Lowest co-pay. Lower cost, commonly used drugs.

Tier 2 (nonpreferred generic): Low co-pay. Category includes most generic drugs.

Tier 3 (preferred brand): Medium co-pay. Many common brand name drugs, called preferred brands, and some higher-cost generic drugs.

Tier 4 (nonpreferred brand): Highest co-pay. Nonpreferred generic and nonpreferred brand name drugs.

Tier 5 (specialty tier): Coinsurance. Unique or very high cost drugs.

Note: The co-pay for Medicare enrollees is a function of both the Medicare Part D drug payment stage and the drug tier. During stage 3 (the so-called doughnut hole between $2,930 and $4,700 in total drug costs), the Medicare enrollee is responsible for 100 percent of the high drug costs. Even in Stage 4, the stage Medicare calls the "catastrophic coverage stage," the Medicare enrollee may be responsible for 33 percent of costs of Tier 4 and Tier 5 drugs. If a single drug costs $1,500 per month, the Medicare enrollee's cost is $500 per month. Although the doughnut hole costs are reducing, this will happen over an extended period of time.

As you can see, Medicare Part D has some real financial drawbacks. Don't worry, though. There are ways to get better coverage, but the fact is, those options will cost you money as well. There is no free ride for most retirees, which is why costs tend to drive decisions. With a limited fixed income, you might feel pushed to make unwise choices, but if you feel this way, you need to take a breath. As noted, options do exist. Chances are there is one for you that will work out to your best advantage.

A few words on preauthorization for Medicare procedures

Typical health care insurance providers require authorization for procedures, often through a referral from a primary care physician to a specialist. No preauthorization is required for reimbursement of physicians, hospitals, and other entities under Medicare Parts A and B. The primary requirement is that the procedure or treatment be medically necessary. Bear in mind that preauthorization is typically required for Medicare Advantage plans (Part C) and Medicare supplement plans.

Medicare supplement plans

As you sort through the various pieces of the health care puzzle you are facing (or will face as you grow older), it's important to relax and take things one step at a time. If you haven't retired yet and need to make choices, take it slow and easy. I'd give you the same advice if you are already retired, but you'll have to act within the open enrollment rules associated with changes in coverage.

As any rate, Medicare supplement plans represent still another arrow in your quiver. These plans are bought to "supplement" your Medicare coverage with additional coverage to make up for the gaps. The benefits include the following:

Hospitalization: In addition to paying deductibles and co-pays for short hospital stays and doctor visits, Medicare supplement plans offer the following benefits:

- Payment of additional deductibles in days sixty-one to ninety. Per day deductibles are $289 per day in 2012.

- Payments of additional deductibles during use of the lifetime extended stay coverage of sixty days per lifetime. Deductibles for lifetime extended stay coverage under Medicare Part A in 2012 are $578 per day.
- As much as one full year of extended stay coverage after the lifetime extended stay coverage is exhausted.

To reiterate an important point: Medicare supplement plans provide payment of excess deductible costs of hospital stays between 60 and 150 days plus coverage for 365 additional days after Medicare hospital benefits end. As I've already said, this coverage could mean the difference between financial ruin and getting through a very difficult time without going broke.

Medical expenses: Part B coinsurance (generally 20 percent of Medicare-approved expenses) or co-payments for hospital outpatient services. Some Medicare supplement plans require that insureds pay a portion of Part B coinsurance or co-payments. Even then, they pay more than Medicare Advantage plans. Logically, lower cost Medicare supplement plans pay less of the deductibles and co-pays than the most expensive monthly charge for Medicare Supplement Plan Type F. Some Medicare supplement plans pay all deductibles and co-payments, reducing or eliminating the Medicare recipient's exposure to potential large costs for deductibles, co-payments, and extended stays.

In addition, Medicare supplement plans provide the following:

- The first three pints of blood each year (Medicare Advantage plans may or may not pay for this).
- Hospice: Part A deductibles.

Other benefits of Medicare supplement plans that are available include the following:

- Payment of coinsurance for skilled nursing facilities.

- Payment of Part A deductibles ($1,156 for the first sixty-day hospital stay).
- Payment of Part B deductibles ($140 per year in 2012).
- Payment of Part B excess (doctors, etc.).
- Payment for a limited portion of health costs during foreign travel.
- Payment for some medical protection while away from home within the United States. Medicare Advantage plans pay for emergency service while away from home, but they do not pay for routine medical care.
- Payment for services from virtually any doctor that accepts Medicare. Medicare Advantage plans limit geographical area, doctors, and hospitals to affiliated groups.

Most seniors of modest means or better give a good hard look at the various Medicare supplement plans available on the market today. Doing so just makes sense. I'll get more into the differences between Part C Advantage plans and supplement plans in the next chapter.

Signing Up for Medicare

As noted in the section on Medicare Part B above, the initial eligibility period for Medicare Part A and Part B enrollment is the seven-month period that starts three months prior to the person's sixty-fifth birthday month and ends three months after the enrollee's sixty-fifth birthday. For people who turn sixty-five on September 10 of this year, their eligibility period is:

Three months before (June, July, and August) the month of their birthday (September) and three months after (October, November, and December).

Pointer: After the initial enrollment year, changes can be made each year during an open enrollment period. In 2013, the open enrollment period was October 15, 2012, to December 7, 2012. Changes became effective January 1, 2013.

Parting words: If you began this chapter knowing nothing about Medicare, then I imagine you're feeling a little overwhelmed with such a big data dump. However, rest assured you're not the only one who finds the Medicare maze a bit hard to navigate. Once you dip your toe in the pool, you'll find that things sort themselves out. My biggest piece of advice is to learn as much as you can and consult with a specialist who knows Medicare inside out. Remember, Part C Advantage plans can have regional wrinkles, so if you're thinking of buying into one of these plans, you need to find out what is offered in your area, what doctors you can see, and if the drugs you take are on the covered list of the program you select.

Paying for health care needn't be a nightmare. We're all in the same boat. The objective is to make sure the boat doesn't leak or sink. I'll get into some Medicare strategies and comparisons in the next chapter that may help you avoid having to bail when you just want to relax and enjoy the view.

9

Medicare Strategies

Now that you have a basic working knowledge of what Medicare is all about, let's get into the nitty-gritty on which components might work best for you. One reason why Medicare seems to be so complex at first is that it was meant to incorporate as much flexibility as possible into how it provides all sorts of people with essential health care coverage after age sixty-five. "One size fits all" doesn't cut it. We all have different needs and financial resources. Flexibility really matters!

There are three alternative Medicare strategies:

1. Medicare Parts A and B, with or without Part D drug coverage.

2. Medicare Advantage plans that replace Parts A and B coverage (the Part B premium is paid to the government, which pays the Medicare Advantage provider) and generally provide Part D (drug coverage) coverage at no additional cost.

3. Medicare supplement plans, with or without Part D drug coverage.

Choosing Medicare Parts A and B alone

Let's take two hypothetical clients as a case in point. Alex and Elizabeth are highly intelligent and very well-educated people, but they confessed to be completely confused by the complexities of Medicare. The more literature they read, the more confused they become. Sound familiar?

I explained that a very high percentage of Medicare eligible people have just Medicare Parts A and B because:

- They believe that the combination of Medicare Parts A and B provides the same coverage they had prior to retiring.
- They do not feel they can afford additional coverage.
- They do not believe they need Part D coverage.

The insurance industry distinguishes between risk assumption and risk avoidance. Clients choosing not to insure for drug costs are assuming the risk, which I think is just simply nuts. Naturally, when people like Alex and Elizabeth take the ostrich position, burying their heads in sand, it makes my business associate and me very uncomfortable. Risk assumption decisions should be made on a cost versus benefits basis, not on a knee-jerk response to what up front seems to be a big bill that doesn't require payment. We strongly believe that the costs of a Part D plan are greatly outweighed by its large potential benefits. The cost of Part D drug coverage for Alex and Elizabeth would be between $40 and $100 each per month.

The retiree's mistake in failing to adequately insure against all kinds of health care risks, not just drug coverage, is far more likely to result in financial ruin for two primary reasons:

1. Retirees don't have future income to recover from medical disasters.

2. The medical costs of health concerns for seniors are

typically much higher than the medical needs of "twentysomethings."

Alex and Elizabeth expressed the rationale for choosing Parts A and B alone as follows: "If we do not currently require any expensive drugs or medical procedures, why should we pay for what we do not use? We're just not up for the extra bills." I told them that the vast majority of people who skimp on health care in planning and managing their retirement end up regretting it later. The risks of financial devastation are simply too great. Just think about the costs of an extended hospital stay. The risk of that happening to you or your spouse without adequate coverage ought to keep you up at night. I know I'd need a sleep aid if I were silly enough to put myself in that position, and yet people do it all the time, possibly because they haven't been privy to the right advice. Prescription drugs might not ruin you all at once, but you can die the death of a thousand cuts if you get sick and don't have coverage for the medicine you need.

Pointer: Don't go with just Medicare Parts A and B. If you do, you may set yourself up for a financial fall you might never recover from.

Medicare Advantage plans

Okay, so now that I've gotten your attention, bear with me for a bit while I explain more about Medicare Advantage plans. Up for it? I hope so, because 25 percent of retirees will choose one of these plans, if prevailing trends continue, and there's no reason why that shouldn't be the case. Well, then, here goes.

Plan C (Medicare Advantage plans) replaces Medicare Parts A and B. Over 70 percent of these plans replace all or some of Medicare Part D coverage. That's a good thing, or it can be, except Medicare Advantage plans are not all alike in what is covered, cost, and coverage areas. Medicare Advantage plans are available only in one specific county or region. Medicare Advantage plans only offer nationwide coverage for emergency care, urgent care, and renal dialysis. I always advise clients to carefully research and consider their unique health needs, their choice of retirement areas, and their financial means in selecting a Medicare Advantage plan.

Medicare Advantage plans cover hospital stays and doctor visits, and they may include prescription drug coverage, preventive services, and other benefits including vision, hearing care, and health club memberships. Medicare Advantage plan costs are usually low (there may be no premium cost). These plans link you to a health maintenance organization (HMO) or a preferred provider organization (PPO). You get to choose. Most people choose an HMO or PPO with either no cost or a very low cost. PPO plans provide more flexibility. You choose your doctors and hospitals and don't need a referral to see a specialist.

Pointer: Medicare Advantage plans typically do *not* provide coverage for large deductibles and the co-pays that result when a patient requires critical care.

Just remember that HMOs or insurance companies receive payment from the US government to provide the Medicare services for Medicare Advantage participants. Part B premiums (Part A is usually free) are either deducted from Social Security checks or paid quarterly to the appropriate government agency. HMOs and insurance companies both typically receive more than 100 percent of the government's expected costs (from paying Medicare providers) and have lower costs due to a limited network of preferred providers. HMOs control costs by providing the service directly through their facilities. Private fee-for-service (PFFS) plans limit costs by limiting both networks and service areas.

When you request information on a Medicare Advantage plan, you will be asked where you live. The medical services available will differ from county to county as well as from year to year. These differences depend on what services were successfully negotiated with doctors and medical faculties in that particular county, in that particular year.

Not all Medicare Advantage plans will be available in each county. Hospitals in an area may choose not to participate in, or to "opt out" of, Medicare Advantage plans, preventing anyone from selecting a Medical Advantage plan in that county. As these plans are typically renegotiated each year, the availability of doctors and medical facilities may change each year. In some extreme cases, the Medicare Advantage plan for an area could cease to exist.

As noted, generally Medicare Advantage enrollees may go outside the identified network of providers, but the enrollee may pay a much greater percentage of provider costs. Emergency health care service may be received outside the geographical area and provider network, but to receive normal health care service with minimal costs, enrollees are limited to preferred providers within the designated geographical area. That can be a real bummer if you like to travel; it can also bite you hard in the wallet if you stray out of your designated network.

Pointer: Medicare Advantage HMOs, PFFS plans, and insurance companies typically provide more services at a lower cost to Medicare enrollees than would result if the Medicare enrollee simply added Part D to Medicare Part A and Part B. That's the upside of things, and it's worth considering despite the limitations.

Bear in mind that an increasing number of doctors have chosen not to participate in Medicare. Others may participate but are out-of-network providers for a particular Medicare Advantage plan. That can also make choosing Part C a bit sticky.

Care should be taken to insure that your preferred doctors and hospitals participate in the Medicare Advantage plan's network. Should you go outside the network for medical service, you will pay a higher cost. It is also very important to make sure that your prescriptions are covered by the plan.

Pointer: When considering Medicare Advantage plans, you should compare them with both the basic Parts A and B coverage, plus a Part D drug plan.

Medicare Advantage plans and Medicare supplement plans are controlled by the Center for Medicare and Medicaid Services (CMS), which determines the standard coverage. CMS also makes the rules for advertising and commissions to agents selling Medicare coverage. CMS rules say you can't have Part D coverage in addition to a Medicare Advantage plan, so if a Medicare Advantage plan does not include drug coverage, you will have no drug coverage. You might wonder, then, why a Medicare Advantage plan would offer coverage but exclude prescriptions drugs. You and me both! These lame plans exist, because some suckers will go for the lower price point without thinking about what they're *not* getting. I use the word "sucker" deliberately. One is born every minute, and it's not a surprise that some health care providers go hunting for them. Just make sure you're not the one that gets bagged.

That said, for many Medicare enrollees, these plans are superior to Medicare Parts A and B alone. The average Medicare Advantage plan cost under $40 per month in 2012. Over half the plans are no-cost plans. Over 70 percent of Medicare Advantage plans provide all or some Part D coverage. As I said, about 25 percent of Medicare participants go for Part C Medicare Advantage plans, so this route may be a viable option for you as well.

A few words on the pros and cons of Medicare Advantage plans

Medicare Advantage plan coverage can beat basic Parts A and B combined with Part D.

Advantages

- Medicare Advantage plans generally have low or no monthly premiums.

- Medicare Advantage plans provide more benefits than the simple combination of Medicare Part A and Part B.
- You can generally enroll with preexisting conditions (the only exception is end-stage renal disease).

Additional advantages may include the following:

- Part D drug coverage
- lower doctor co-pays
- reduced deductibles
- hearing, vision, and fitness benefits
- wellness coverage

Disadvantages

- Plans are annual contracts, and benefits may change; premiums and co-payments may increase. Plans may decide not to negotiate or renew their contracts.
- There may be higher annual out-of-pocket expenses than under traditional Medicare.
- Under some Medicare Advantage plans, you may find it hard to find medical care while traveling. Medicare Advantage plans cover emergency care but not routine or normal care.
- Medicare Advantage plan benefits are more limited than participants may believe. Participants typically don't even understand deductibles and co-pays. Even those who understand deductibles and co-pays almost never understand term limits for hospital stays.
- Rules may prevent medical care from being covered (e.g., located outside coverage area or care considered not medically necessary).
- Deductibles and co-pays from a Medicare Advantage plan, especially during extended hospital stays, may result in higher costs than a Medicare supplement plan combined with Medicare Parts A, B, and D.

- Indigent seniors may have higher costs than they would under combined Medicare and Medicaid plans. They should utilize either low income programs or Medicaid to pay costs Medicare might not pay. (I have a big problem with the ethics of selling these people Medicare Advantage plans.)
- Medicare Advantage plans have limited choices of hospitals, doctors, and other medical care providers.
- Continuity of care may be interrupted for patients whose doctors opt out of the Medicare Advantage plan.

Medicare supplement plans

Medicare supplement plans, also known as Medigap plans, may initially appear more costly than Medicare Advantage plans, but they are far more flexible, may have more coverage, and reduce the out-of-pocket costs in co-pays and deductibles. The cost of a premium Medicare supplement plus Part D coverage is about $200 per person per month in 2012. Still sound too steep?

Well, think about this for a minute or two. What would you do if you or your spouse faced an extended hospital stay and you only signed up for basic Medicare Part A and Part B? Or how about a cheap Medicare Advantage plan? Both traditional Medicare Part A and Medicare Advantage plans replacing Part A can result in financial ruin if an extended hospital stay is required, because you're simply not covered or the co-pays and deductibles continue to mount the longer you're stuck in the hospital. In other words, you're going to get hit with the tab if something bad happens. Your Medicare supplement plan can help protect you against exposure to extreme financial risk, so give buying such a plan a heck of a lot of thought before you decide to go with a less expensive and less comprehensive Medicare Advantage plan.

A key point of comparison

Medicare supplement plans work in *conjunction* with Medicare Parts A, B, and D, which means you've still got to pay for Part B and Part D if you want the best possible coverage, including payments for your prescription drugs. By contrast, Medicare Advantage plans *replace* Medicare Parts A, B, and D. Many seniors choose Medicare Advantage plans because they provide coverage at little or no cost beyond paying the required Medicare Part B cost. Medicare supplement insurance helps pay for Medicare deductibles and co-pays.

Pointer: Medicare supplement insurance becomes more costly the later it is elected and may even be unavailable subject to insurability issues if delayed beyond the initial three years of Medicare eligibility.

Medical insurability for all parts is generally not required in the first three years of Medicare eligibility. Those delaying coverage may encounter eligibility issues. However, insurability standards for Medicare may be much easier to meet than individual health insurance standards, even when there is delayed enrollment. If a participant can afford the relatively low additional costs to buy *both* a Medicare supplement plan *and* a Part D drug plan (typically $200 to $300 per month), the benefits greatly exceed the costs.

Benefits include substantial reduction of the potential for financial ruin that typically accompanies extended hospital stays, and protection of a participant's spouse from financial ruin following such a hospital stay. Most working individuals will recognize that even the highest quality Medicare supplement plan (Plan F for most participants) plus Part D drug coverage is both much less expensive and better than all but the very best corporate plans.

Going for the best

So are you getting a clue as to which Medicare strategy I most fully support? I thought so. Buying a premium Medicare supplement plan plus Part D coverage maximizes the chance to maintain your financial assets and quality of life. The approximately $200 per person per month in addition to the Medicare Part B monthly premium cost is meager compared to the value.

Those who pay for coverage they do not use should not feel they wasted the money, but rather that they eliminated or reduced a catastrophic exposure. I also remind you that when a person first qualifies for Medicare, there is no exclusion for preexisting conditions.

A few words on timing

You can only make the change to a Medicare supplement plan during open enrollment dates for that year. In 2012, the open enrollment period was October 15 to December 7.

Note therefore that the best time for a Medicare eligible person to make the decision to buy a Medicare supplement plan is in the year of initial eligibility, when they have the seven-month window beginning three months prior to their birth month and ending three months after their birth month.

A handy dandy Medicare comparison table

So just in case you needed a little more data to chew on, here's a comparison table for you to consider. Take a good hard look at the information. It may help you decide which course of action best fits your wallet and your risk tolerance.

Medicare Plan Comparisons

Doctor and hospital choice is any that will accept Medicare Parts A and B and Medicare supplements. Restrictions to in-network service can be pretty restrictive for Medicare Advantage.

	Medicare Part A & B	Medicare Advantage	Medicare Supplement
Hospitalization			
Days 1–60	All but $1,156	$295 per day	What A & B doesn't cover
		Co-pay first 5 days	
		What A & B doesn't cover	
		Days 6–60	
61–90	All but $289/day	What A & B doesn't cover	What A & B doesn't cover
91—60 days lifetime is used up	All but $578/day	What A & B doesn't cover	What A & B doesn't cover
After using 90 days plus lifetime 60 days	Nothing	What A & B doesn't cover	All for one year
Blood			
First 3 pints	Nothing		For 3 pints
Hospice Care			
	Nearly all		The rest
Medical Services, Including Doctors			
First $140 of Medicare approved amounts	Nothing		The rest
Remainder of Medicare approved amounts	Generally 80%	The rest	The rest
Part B Excess Charges (above Medicare approved amounts)			
Blood: First 3 pints	Nothing		The rest
Durable Medical Equipment			
First $140 of Medicare approved amounts	Nothing		The rest
Remainder of Medicare approved amounts	Generally 80%		The rest
Foreign Travel			
First $250 per calendar year	Nothing		Nothing
Remainder of charges	Nothing		80% up to $50,000

Parting words: Seniors with very low incomes will typically prefer Medicare Advantage plans, as they feel they cannot afford the Medicare supplement costs. The risk of Medicare Advantage plans is the significantly greater cost exposure as the taxpayer gets older and increasingly frail. Thus, I generally suggest Medicare supplement plans, where needs appear imminent or where financial means to pay higher premiums exist.

The Medicare supplement plan costs influence the decisions of the majority of both "do-it-yourselfers" and salespeople. The sales pitch is much easier in no-cost Medicare Advantage plans, thus many salespeople only attempt to sell Medicare Advantage plans, even though there are huge coverage gaps compared with Medicare supplement plans. Consultants like me almost always prefer Medicare supplement plans, because we view the benefits from choosing a Medicare supplement plan to *far* outweigh the monthly expense.

10

Drawing Down Smart

YOU'VE PROBABLY WORKED ALL your life to get what you have, and now you just want to stop working and enjoy yourself while you're still healthy and have all your marbles. That's the story, and you're sticking to it. Great! That's as it should be. However, as you ride off into the brilliant orange ball of a rising sun (notice I didn't say setting sun), you need to get your cash flow priorities configured so you can actually have a good time without stressing over your finances. Accomplishing that objective isn't impossible. Frankly, doing so is an achievable goal even if you have a somewhat limited asset pool.

I've been shouting from my soapbox about the importance of cash flow throughout this book, and I'm not about to stop now. Cash flow is king. Assets allow for cash flow, but only if you have the right allocation of income-producing investments in addition to your Social Security and possibly a corporate or government pension. Figuring out how to draw those investments down, or to preserve or even grow them, is a major concern, especially since we're living longer (if we're lucky), cruising through life in our midnineties like it was yesterday's gold watch time at sixty-five. Get the cash flow equation right, and you sleep soundly at night. Get it wrong, and, well, uh, let's just not go there!

Tax laws, Social Security rules, and Medicare rules change. Review plans periodically and consider seeking a specialist's opinion in addition to your normal tax or financial professional. Retirees who refuse to study the issues and adapt to required changes in their thought process may experience problems unnecessarily. Retirees find it difficult to grow their cash flow. They need to know that future cash flows can outpace future cash outflows, but the only way to do that is with sound planning and ongoing cash flow management as things change.

So with the cash flow model firmly in mind, let's take a look at some key strategies regarding how you can make what you have work harder for you. The first thing you need to evaluate is where you want to live. According to AARP, the vast majority of retirees stay in the region where they worked and raised their families. They may abandon the traditional neighborhood in favor of an active adult community, where they'll find people of a similar age, plenty of activities, and no need to cut the grass, but they're not migrating to the Sunbelt like people once did. However, the current crowd of upcoming retiree boomers is also mindful of taxes, and a steady stream of us is funneling into states where Social Security isn't taxed, where pension income is taxed less, and where property taxes are low. These folks are bucking the AARP-identified trend of staying in place, even if property taxes are through the roof, because they're mindful of drains on limited cash flow.

Pretty smart, eh?

Home is where your wallet is

Some states do not tax any income, and others provide tax breaks for retirees. There are nine states with no state income tax under current law:

1. Alaska

2. Florida

3. Nevada

4. New Hampshire

5. South Dakota

6. Texas

7. Tennessee

8. Washington

9. Wyoming

New Hampshire and Tennessee, however, tax dividends and interest. None of the other seven states tax dividends and interest.

South Carolina, which does have a state income tax, doesn't tax Social Security, it provides big breaks on property taxes on a primary residence for people over the age of sixty-five, and it currently waives state income taxes on the first fifteen grand of pension income for people over the age of sixty-five. South Carolina is considered a retirement-friendly state, even though it has a state income tax. The point is you've got to look at all the factors when deciding to relocate to enhance your cash flow by reducing your tax liabilities. Your quality of life is important too. Just because a state like Florida doesn't tax your income doesn't mean it's totally friendly to retirees; you need to consider property taxes, homeowner's insurance rates, and personal property taxes on cars, boats, and other tangible assets.

There are other states like South Carolina. Georgia, for example, grants tax breaks for individuals age sixty-two and older. Georgia taxes earned income but grants significant tax relief for unearned income of persons over sixty-two. Other states offer tax breaks for senior citizens. Some portion of retirement income is nontaxable in approximately 25 percent of the states. Advisers and family members should be cognizant of which states offer these advantages. Many famous athletes and entertainers choose their state of residence to reduce income taxes, but this issue is frequently ignored by advisers when clients plan retirement.

A few words on pensions

Cash flow, *not* assets, should be viewed as the central premise (variable) for planning retirement. Sufficient cash flow allows retirees to

- meet physiological (food, shelter, and health care) needs,
- buy Medicare Part D drug coverage and Medicare supplement insurance or elect an appropriate Medicare Advantage plan, and
- interact socially with friends and family.

Corporate and government pensions sometimes offer a choice between cash flow for life, in the form of a monthly income, and a lump sum. Most corporate pensions do not index for cost of living, while most government pensions are indexed for inflation. When given a choice, I frequently advise taking the monthly government pension, but typically I advise taking the lump sum from corporate pensions, which seldom provide cost of living protection. Each situation has to be analyzed carefully on its own merits.

Maximize your tax deferrals

Tax rules limit deferrals per calendar year, not per calendar month! Taxpayers should make every effort to make maximum deferrals in their last working years. If investors do not have excess cash flow to make the deferrals, they should consider utilizing an equity loan to make the deferrals. Home equity loans may provide a means to delay drawing Social Security, variable annuities with living benefits, and cash flow from nontraded REITs.

Another way to go would be to reduce your emergency funds for a few years to maximize available cash flow. Strategic thinking is essential if you're to come out on top of the retirement game.

Deferring deductible retirement contributions may have the following positive effects on retirement income:

a. Current tax rates are typically higher than or equal to retirement tax rates.

b. If one is in a combined marginal (federal and state) tax rate of 25 percent, then for every $4 deferred, the retirement account grows $5 ($4 deferred plus $1 tax deferral).

Pointer: It makes sense to put off taking tax-deferred dollars from your portfolio for as long as possible. Get cash flow from other assets first, if you can swing it.

That's why I suggest that you might want to consider establishing an equity line of credit, even if you do not currently have a need. The time to do this is just before you retire. Here is the rationale:

1. An equity loan can supplement emergency funds, reducing the likelihood of making poor decisions during retirement.

2. Once earned income decreases due to retirement, it becomes much more difficult to qualify for an equity loan.

3. Equity loans are a very low cost of capital in a low interest rate environment.

4. Equity loans may be used to replace short-term cash flow when maximizing contributions to qualified retirement plans during the last working years.

5. Equity loans can also be used to defer drawing down tax-deferred assets.

6. Equity loans may be used to reduce higher cost debt. Note that this increases both current and future cash flows.

You might think my idea is a bit radical. Who borrows money when they have assets to draw upon? The point is, you have more options than you may think when it comes to deciding on which assets to use first in your retirement planning. Deferring taxes can save you more than it costs to get an equity loan, depending on your tax rate. Keep an open mind and always think strategically. Besides, your home is an asset. It could possibly be the biggest one you have.

What to draw down and when

Choosing assets to draw down in retirement should begin with assets whose value does not fluctuate. Thus, prefer cash and money markets for drawing down each year. Prior to the year, make sure there is enough cash to draw for the entire year. Having the next year's required funds in a money market is a safeguard.

First steps: Financial professionals often suggest clients reduce their nonqualified (taxable) investments for the short period between retirement and the beginning of Social Security benefits. This period is frequently labeled the "drawdown period," because nonqualified assets are reduced to meet cash flow shortfalls caused by deferring Social Security benefits. Contrary to common opinion, I suggest that if you've got to spend money in the short term to get the most out of Social Security by deferring it to full retirement age or age seventy, go for the liquid taxable assets first. Covet those tax-deferred accounts. Their tax-deferred status makes them very valuable.

Pointer: Restrict illiquid investments to approximately one-third or less of your portfolio.

Balancing income needs with asset accumulation and retention can be very difficult. Advisers and seniors should perform two distinct sets of calculations.

Set #1 should evaluate all cash flows and assets based upon cash needs.

This calculation helps determine whether assets need to be converted for income production. Ideally, cash flow will be sufficient to meet day-to-day needs, and assets can be allowed to grow to provide a margin of safety and to combat the erosive effects of inflation.

Set #2 should convert all monthly income sources, including pensions and Social Security, to expected economic value over life expectancy.

A pension of $60,000 for a life expectancy of twenty years might be worth $600,000 in today's dollars. Failure to incorporate monthly cash flows into equivalent economic value may result in very bad decisions. For example, retirees with a monthly corporate or government pension (including Social Security) may have adequate monthly cash flow but lack easily liquidated assets for emergency needs.

As an aside, I would be very reluctant to recommend a fixed or variable annuity for the above individual. Another client might have substantial assets but only a small monthly Social Security check. I would be much more likely to recommend an appropriate annuity for that individual. Overcoming the client's anxiety over the possibility of outliving their income is a very real need, and it cannot be addressed by advisers who fail to understand the difference between the appropriate approach for the distribution stage of retirement and the accumulation stage.

It is very important to balance cash flow needs and the need for liquid assets. All monthly cash flows and assets should be considered in determining an appropriate mix. Some assets may be selected to provide cash flow, while others provide long-term security in exchange for less liquidity.

Drawing ready cash first often makes sense

Nowadays, many of my clients have large cash balances in money market accounts that are earning practically zero interest, and yet they will think nothing of drawing $1,000 a month from a $40,000 IRA that could be earning 4 percent. Thus, they are depleting principal and incurring additional tax liabilities when they could avoid both by drawing down their liquid assets, currently moldering away in the money market account. This is why I suggested earlier that you should buck common advice during your near-term drawdown period and hit the liquid taxable assets first, holding the tax-deferred (qualified) assets in reserve for later.

To illustrate:

If you draw $12,000 from your IRA worth $40,000, you will typically owe combined federal and state taxes of at least 20 percent. Thus, your net from the $12,000 is only $9,600. Now, let's say you didn't spend the $9,600 and instead kept it invested at 4 percent, which is about the norm these days if you invest wisely. You would earn $384 in taxable cash flow on the after-tax net. If you drew only earnings from the IRA at 4 percent on the $12,000, you'd earn $480. Thus, the earnings/cash flow cost is $96 per year, or the difference between the $480 you could have had and the $384 you ended up with. If you multiply the magnitude of this difference by tens of thousands of dollars, you can see that drawing down one asset versus another can have some serious cash flow consequences.

The above scenario is a tragic mistake that even bright people make. They reason that they have to pay taxes eventually and don't understand that the longer they utilize the tax advantage of the IRA/retirement account, the more cash flow they earn from their investment. The bottom line is that the eventual asset value is the same, but until they withdraw the money, they earn and can receive cash flow on the unpaid taxes resulting from deferral. In other words, you'd have the $480 to spend instead of the $384.

Pointer: Consider the cost of all cash flow sources, including home equity loans and drawing down investments, before deciding which sources to utilize first in meeting cash flow needs.

Your Roth IRA is a great tool for you and your heirs

Senior taxpayers with Roth IRAs should generally distribute those assets only after all other assets have been liquidated. Their heirs will be able to distribute the Roth account with no tax due on either earnings or principal proportionately over the heirs' remaining life expectancy. Senior taxpayers with little or no income should either convert their IRAs to Roth or draw them down first to pay medical and other expenses. They will incur either no tax or much less tax than their heirs would incur if they inherit a taxable IRA. In short, don't spend your Roth IRA money first!

Seniors should consider both their own tax circumstances and their heirs' tax situation if they expect to leave a legacy for their children. Many seniors have little or no taxable income due to both reduced income and higher deductible medical costs. If these seniors have IRAs, they should consider converting the IRAs to Roth IRAs. The seniors' low tax bracket will result in very little tax being paid, but their children who would inherit the IRA might be in a much higher tax bracket, leaving them with a much smaller net inheritance.

Annuities are also taxed very unfavorably to heirs. I typically lean more toward alternative investments, especially nontraded public REITs, if I suspect the senior will be leaving a legacy. The very best retirement advisers consider a wide range of factors. Failure to consider taxes is both negligent and lazy, in my opinion.

A few words on sequence risk

Financial security and the quality of the retirement experience are dependent upon timing your retirement properly. Sadly, most people don't think about timing at all. When they're eligible for Social Security and they have enough time logged in on the job to qualify for a pension (if they're very lucky), they bolt out the door. Yet timing is everything, as they say.

Consider those retirees who retired in either of the following time periods:

a. 1999, at the height of the dot.com bubble, into 2002 when the bubble burst

b. mid-2007, when the recession first began to show, through 2009, when the stock market began to reveal faint signs of life again

Clearly, you can't have a crystal ball to predict future bulls and bears on Wall Street. If you could, you'd be fabulously wealthy. So without the ability to see into the future, these two groups of retirees got slammed in two of the worst market downturns on record. As a consequence, they probably grossly misjudged the adequacy of their assets and income/cash flow because they based their decisions on current market conditions, without building in the margin of safety I keep harping on in these pages. Many of these seniors now struggle to make ends meet, and some have returned to work. Very few managed to restore their prior income. Thus, they worry for their own and their spouse's financial future. They retired with little or no insight into the importance of the sequence of investment returns during the portion of retirement after distributions.

I tell clients considering retirement that they must carefully consider whether they have a sufficient margin of safety to ensure that they don't retire too early and encounter an unfriendly investment era. Just as important, or perhaps even more so, if you see the market is trending down and there's financial trouble in the wind, think twice, no, think a dozen times before you pull the trigger on retirement. Once you're out the door, you probably won't be able to come back under the same terms. So if you take a look around and don't like the investment environment, don't make any rash decisions. Look before you leap!

Let's take a quick look at the nature of sequence risks. Note the difference in assets after a mere five years between cases 1 and 2; these people retired based upon investments of $400,000 with annual income needs of $20,000. If the first five years investment returns are:

Case 1 return

Yr 1 -9%
Yr 2 -11%
Yr 3 -22%
Yr 4 +25%
Yr 5 +11%
Remaining assets = $239,747

The order of investment returns in retirement is sometimes called sequencing risk. Financial products have even been developed to reduce or ameliorate this risk. Note the incredible difference for case 2, where the year 1 returns were the same as case 1's year 4 returns, and the year 5 returns were the same as year 3 returns, and years 3–5 were the same as years 1–3. Cases 1 and 2 had exactly the same investment returns but in different order:

Case 2 return

Yr 1 +25%
Yr 2 +11%
Yr 3 -9%
Yr 4 -11%
Yr 5 -22%
Remaining assets = $274,463

The difference is $34,716, or 14 percent. For this reason, prior to retirement I typically advise clients to make appropriate portfolio adjustments. These portfolio adjustments are not just the obvious suggestion to raise the percentage allocation to fixed income.

Classic investment advice would suggest raising the allocation to fixed income when clients begin retirement. While it is still appropriate to lower the equity allocation at retirement, seniors, their advisers, and their loved ones should be aware that there are financial products, created in response to volatility and poor equity returns of the last twelve years, that can be utilized to provide greater retirement security. Taking advantage of variable annuities and traded and nontraded real estate investment trusts are just two examples.

Asset allocations matter

Just to remind you, retirement asset allocation refers to the process of determining what portion of your retirement investments are allocated to each investment type. While there is no consensus, research suggests that the less comfortable you expect to be in retirement, the greater the allocation should be to portions that provide consistent, reliable income. For example, if you are lucky enough to have a retirement pension that, combined with Social Security, meets your basic retirement needs, you may be advised to allocate a greater portion of your remaining assets to growth assets, and if you need considerable income beyond Social Security, you should primarily invest your retirement assets to supplement your Social Security income.

The above advice sounds perfectly logical, doesn't it? You'd be amazed at how few people apply that logic. To repeat: Does it make sense to keep all your assets in low-returning fixed income investments if your pension and Social Security provide enough cash flow to meet your needs? Of course not. But the traditional advice would tell you to do just that, to reduce risk. I argue that a sense of balance between risk and choice of asset allocation is far more likely to make you feel comfortable and happy during your retirement.

Pointer: The goal of retirement portfolio allocations should be to maximize return potential for a given level of risk. Risk tolerance defines both the appropriate investment mix and the potential cash flow and asset growth.

Finally, try to focus on investments and other channels for cash flow that will increase over time to combat the erosive effects of inflation. Remember the big P in the CAMP score we discussed earlier? Maximizing future purchasing power is a vital component of retirement planning and management.

The following table lists many instruments that have some degree of inflation protection; others listed in the table do not.

Retirement Vehicle	Cash Flow Increases When This Happens
Social Security	Inflation Occurs or Benefits Are Delayed
Stocks	Corporate Revenues Grow, Increasing Dividends
Corporate Bonds	Almost Never
Treasury Bonds	Never
Treasury Inflation-Protected Securities (TIPSs)	Cash Flow Doesn't Increase but Principal Grows with Inflation
Federal Pensions	Inflation Occurs or Benefits Are Delayed
State Pensions	Inflation Occurs or Benefits Are Delayed (No Index in Some States)
Local Pensions	A Very Few Are Inflation Indexed
Corporate Pensions	A Very Few Are Inflation Indexed
Stock Mutual Funds	Corporate Revenues Grow, Increasing Dividends
Bond Mutual Funds	Slowly When Interest Rates Rise, but Principal May be Lost
Fixed Annuities/CDs	Slowly When Interest Rates Rise
Variable Annuities	Cash Flows Rise Based upon Delayed Receipt and Increasing Mutual Fund Values
Nontraded REITs	Rents Grow and Dividends Are Reinvested, Increasing Future Dividends

A few words about life insurance

Although I don't consider life insurance as an investment, certain policyholders do have cash flow options that are worth a good look. Here are five instances where life insurance might make sense for you:

1. To provide income replacement for spouse or dependent on the premature death of the income earner

2. To replace assets if asset principal (in addition to income) is to be used to meet monthly cash flow needs

3. To ensure the adequacy of assets to produce cash flow on the premature death of one member of a couple, especially if one member has a pension that terminates on their death that would negatively impact on existing cash flow

4. To protect dependents who are unable to care for themselves, such as an elderly parent or a special-needs child (one-third of American households have a special-needs child)

5. To provide a small death benefit with a long-term care rider to guard against nursing home and home care expenses (more on this in the next chapter)

The real rub is, significant life insurance coverage can cost you a fortune when you're older, and you might not be able to get it at all if you have preexisting conditions that would cause an underwriter to back away. So what do you do? Let's look at what's out there.

Term-insurance policies

Term life insurance is what is says. You buy the insurance for a "term," and it is in effect until it expires. Sometimes you need to take a physical exam, and sometimes you don't. This type of insurance for older boomers is typically appropriate only if the need for insurance will end on or about the end of the contract, which usually covers the insured for ten or fifteen years. The older you are when you buy, the more the premiums are going to cost, because the company will see you as an increasing risk. If you're planning to retire and you see a gap in cash flow that could occur early on in the event of your death, say while you are working to make up a shortfall due to deferring Social Security, then buying a term-life insurance policy early that will cover the time period of greatest risk makes a lot of sense.

Getting coverage in your eighties will be out of reach for most people. Odds of preexisting conditions that prevent underwriting the policy will increase exponentially. Life expectancy goes way down once you hit your eighties, so insurance companies aren't all that interested in wagering on you from an actuarial standpoint. Yet in cases of a lucrative pension terminating on the death of one spouse, leaving the other financially stranded without sufficient cash flow to meet daily needs, the extra expense of a fifteen-year term-life policy bought in your late sixties may be merited, assuming you can get one. Only you can decide if you need insurance of this kind, how much you're willing (or can afford) to pay, and how much coverage is worth having.

Term-life insurance policies can be extended beyond the contract expiration date, but the premiums skyrocket. Usually, if you want to continue coverage, you have to buy a new policy just before the contract on your current policy expires. That means if you hit your seventies or eighties and go looking to buy another term-life insurance policy, you might very well be out of luck. That's one main reason why I don't encourage retirees to bank on term-life insurance as a part of their retirement finances.

Term-life insurance policies for funerals

Some insurance companies offer term-life insurance policies to pay for funeral expenses, saying that there is no physical examination and that preexisting conditions don't matter. Just bear in mind that the amount of coverage is usually very small, and that the fine print for more extensive coverage does indeed say you may have to submit to a physical exam and that some preexisting conditions exclude you. If it sounds too good to be true, it probably is. Relatively speaking, premiums for these insurance plans are quite high.

If you know you'll be living close to the limit of your cash flow when you retire, then buying a funeral policy that pays out $10,000 or so to cover funeral expenses might make sense, especially if you don't have liquid assets to draw upon in the sad event of a spouse's death. If you know things will be tight after you retire, perhaps you shouldn't retire at all. If you go ahead anyway, then consider prepaying for funeral expenses before you stop collecting a regular paycheck so that you can make back the cash you spent to hedge against the inevitable. Reputable funeral homes will put the money into an interest-bearing account that should keep up with inflation, so when the time comes, you or your spouse won't have to worry about making arrangements and paying the bills associated with the burial or cremation. Nobody likes to plan his or her own funeral, but such planning does factor into your retirement strategy, whether you like it or not.

Term-life insurance for mortgage protection

Most experts agree that buying a term-life policy to pay off a mortgage in case the household's key earner dies prematurely is usually not a great use of funds. If the earner is older, premiums will be high. Odds are the earner won't die within the term of the contract anyway, so premiums will be wasted. Mortgage protection should not be the sole purpose of the policy. Putting a life insurance benefit toward paying off a mortgage does make sense in some cases, but don't buy just because you have a mortgage.

Whole-life insurance

Whole-life insurance is what it means. The insurance company agrees to insure you for your entire life. You pay into the policy, and the benefits increase over time. You also accrue cash value.

With whole-life, the company knows it's going to pay on the policy eventually, assuming you don't cash out of the program (as many people do). Underwriting is usually very strict, requiring applicants to be in good or adequate health. The older you are, the harder it is to qualify for the extensive coverage of most whole-life insurance policies. The policy will also command much higher premiums, some to the point where they are beyond the reach of even modestly wealthy seniors. The flip side is, if you buy such a policy when you're young and fit, and you can afford to keep up the premiums no matter what, then a whole-life policy can be an excellent arrow to have in your financial quiver.

Once you have the contract, the company can't cancel it, as long as you pay the premiums. If you develop a physical condition that would otherwise exclude you, you're still covered. Some policies even will pay if you commit suicide, as long as you don't do it right away. You can typically borrow against the policy, if necessary. You can often assign ownership of the policy to heirs. Whole-life policies earn cash value (face value) and pay guaranteed dividends. They also pay nonguaranteed dividends that promise more than the guaranteed dividends, which makes the policy attractive from an investment perspective. The insurance agent will tell you that with whole life, you're not throwing your premiums away, like you are with term life. In many senses, they are right.

Pointer: The agent may also say the policy will pay for itself once the cash value hits a specified threshold. Don't hold your breath. Companies change the deal all the time. Buy only if you can afford the premiums forever.

The downside of whole life is, the premiums can cost thousands of dollars per year for even $200,000 or $300,000 of coverage, and that's if you buy early. Whole-life insurance policies providing large amounts of coverage (several hundred thousand dollars or more) are generally thought of as instruments of the affluent. Whole-life insurance policies offering smaller amounts of coverage could be an excellent and affordable buffer, if you think you need it to help your spouse deal with cash flow over a limited time period after your death.

As noted, if you have a special-needs child who will likely outlive you, whole-life insurance could be appropriate. Ditto if you or your spouse will be left out in the cold if a pension terminates on death. And here's a really big consideration: long-term care.

Whole-life insurance may be used as a source of cash flow in retirement. For example, life insurance with a long-term care rider is very appropriate to ensure that a lasting illness does not deplete assets for the surviving spouse. Ironically, many advisers assume that single seniors need long-term care insurance more than a couple does. These sources ignore the devastating effect upon the survivor of a lingering illness for the first to die. I believe married couples need life insurance with a long-term care rider to ensure against such financially ruinous events. I'll get into this subject in the next chapter.

Parting words: Drawing down is actually a scary term, because it implies that you're spending your savings. Most of us would prefer not to draw our assets down, and some of us can manage to do just that with the right basket of investments, maximized Social Security benefits, and a corporate or government pension. Others will have to slowly spend principal because they face shortages in cash flow, a very dangerous circumstance since life expectancy is extending for many of us into our ninth decade. The bottom line is, there are plenty of options for you to think about and pursue. Keep focused on ways to enhance cash flow. Don't put too much emphasis on liquidity and asset retention at the cost of cash flow. With the right financial planning and management, you can enjoy a comfortable and happy retirement.

II

Outfoxing the Bogeyman

THE IDEA OF LIVING out the rest of our lives in a nursing home is repellent at best. Add the potentially devastating financial consequences to the equation, and it's easy to see why future and current retirees just don't want to consider the subject of long-term care (LTC). I can understand that. At times, I feel the same way, and I'm a certified long-term care professional, charged with the often unpleasant duty of filling my clients in on the issues. The whole thing is just too hard to bear—the deterioration of body and mind, the paying down of assets you worked your entire life to acquire, the impoverishment of your spouse, the complete loss of the estate so your kids get nothing.

It's a potentially sad story indeed, but it doesn't have to be. There are ways for you to protect yourself and your spouse. Before I get into your options, let's first take a quick look at the basics of the current sobering reality on the ground, dispelling some common myths along the way, like the one that says Medicare covers long-term care. It doesn't, or at least hardly anything.

According to recent data from Morningstar, family and friends provide 78 percent of all long-term care, and thirty-nine million Americans currently provide care for someone over age fifty. Approximately 40 percent of us will require some form of long-term care during our lifetimes. Some sources say only 25 percent of us will need long-term care, while others say it's more like 75 percent for seniors over the age of sixty-five. Either way you cut it, the scary fact remains that it's statistically probable that you or your spouse will need some sort of long-term care at a given time in your lives, most likely at the end. In 2010, 25 percent of all deaths in America occurred in nursing homes, according to Morningstar. Now if that's not depressing, I don't know what is.

The costs for long-term care provided by a nursing home vary, but it's expensive no matter where you live. Morningstar's data pegs the median annual costs for long-term care in a nursing home at $73,000. Statistics differ, sometimes widely, but it doesn't take a rocket scientist to figure out that the bugaboo of long-term care is definitely looming large in modern American society.

Complex factors influencing long-term care costs include the following:

- length of LTC needs
- quality of LTC assistance
- severity of LTC needs
- region of the United States

LTC costs frequently escalate during periods of physical frailty. Increasing physical frailty is almost inevitable when we live longer lives. Ironically, medical advances that prevent premature death also increase the likelihood for needing LTC assistance. It's important to note that long-term care differs from medical care. Long-term care refers to assistance in what are known as the six activities of daily living (ADLs). In other words, if you need help to do basic things you're a long-term care candidate.

Activities of daily living

- eating
- continence (the control of bodily functions, both urinary and fecal)

- dressing
- bathing
- toileting (requiring assistance with elimination needs)
- transferring (walking)

There is a distinction between the medical definitions of toileting and continence; someone who is incontinent cannot control their bodily functions. Toileting refers to assisting a person who may be able to control bodily functions but needs help with any of the following:

- ambulatory assistance
- bedpan
- urinal
- diaper
- catheter

Pointer: Long-term care is defined by the need of assistance with ADLs. Depending on your long-term care coverage, you can receive assistance with your ADLs at home, in an assisted-living facility, or in a skilled nursing setting such as a nursing home.

Medicare won't pay for much long-term care

Very little long-term care assistance is provided under Medicare. Although long-term care assistance is defined as a deductible medical cost for federal tax purposes, it is defined as a personal care cost, *not* a medical cost, for both Medicare and insurance purposes. The distinction is hugely important. Medicare eligible expenses must be medical needs. Therefore, long-term care needs only qualify if they are both medically caused and temporary.

Both tax deductibility and insurance policies require at least standby assistance needs with two or more of the six ADLs. Standby assistance means that someone must be nearby in case assistance is needed. Persons with certain cognitive or mental impairments qualify without establishing either the need for hands-on assistance (a higher standard) or that they need assistance with two or more ADLs. As you can see, things can get complicated fast.

Pointer: Medicare is designed to pay for acute, short-term illnesses. Services are only available to those who need skilled nursing care or therapies.

Note that Medicare pays only for medical assistance from qualified medical personnel. After a three-day hospital stay, Medicare will pay for skilled nursing care for a maximum of a hundred days. After the first twenty days, the amount Medicare pays reduces sharply. Even in the first twenty days, it must be determined that the skilled nursing care will restore the patient's capabilities. If restoration of capabilities is not expected, then Medicare can't be expected to pay. Unfortunately, very few people adequately address the potential financial disaster that can result from needing assistance with the six activities of daily living. The six activities of daily living are critical, because they define the conditions that must exist for long-term care insurance to cover costs, and they define conditions for deducting costs as medical expenses on federal tax returns.

The risks are too high to ignore long-term care

As I've said, failure to adequately provide for the possibility of significant LTC needs not only risks the quality of life of the patient, it also risks the quality of life of their spouse and family members. This is because of the following three factors:

1. Financial assets may be strained or even totally decimated.

2. Stress of caring for the frail person may physically impair other family members and friends.

3. Emotional distress due to the condition of the beloved family member.

Few individuals or couples have the resources to pay for all potential LTC costs from either cash flow or assets. Even those who can afford to pay for LTC should be advised not to accept the risk, as the risk far outweighs the potential savings from self-insuring. Seniors should rely on income from assets to pay for LTC only if the income is not necessary to pay for day-to-day cost-of-living needs. Self-insurance is enticing, but only those with very substantial assets should choose to totally self-insure.

Pointer: Some sources figure the costs of LTC and medical expenses at over $10,000 per month. Thus, you would need an annual income of 5 percent on investment assets of $2.4 million just to meet the projected annual LTC costs of $120,000. Yikes!

And it gets worse: additional assets would be required to meet other costs and needs. Few people have sufficient assets to totally self-insure. Few people have a net worth substantially in excess of the $2.4 million necessary to pay for possible LTC expenses of $120,000 or more, plus meet their other needs.

Even those who do have sufficient assets seldom want to use all those assets, for two critical reasons:

1. They worry about outliving their life expectancy.

2. They want to protect their spouse or heirs from receiving nothing due to a prolonged LTC need.

Pointer: Assets that need to be dedicated to earning the required expenses for meeting potential LTC needs should not be counted when considering assets available for meeting other retirement cash flows.

My business associate and I are firmly convinced that this double counting is done by most advisers and seniors. This unfortunately results in the following statistic: industry and government experts say that fewer than 10 percent of those who may need LTC coverage are adequately covered. One of the most common retirement planning mistakes is asking investments to provide needed cash flow and emergency capital.

In spite of the risks, some people simply cannot afford LTC protection. They need all the income from their investments plus any Social Security or pension just to meet their daily needs. These people may have to have to rely on family members or Medicaid to provide for any LTC needs. Forty percent of Americans who need LTC are below 150 percent of the federal poverty level and therefore must rely on Medicaid, so you're not alone if you end up spending down your assets due to long-term care needs. The number will grow as millions of baby boomers continue to age.

You've got options

Paying for some kind of long-term care coverage is very difficult for many of us. The average cost differs depending on what product you buy, but it's safe to say you've got to have thousands of dollars annually or the ability to fork over a large lump sum for long-term care protection. That said, you do have options that can be tailored to your needs. If you can't afford the full boat, then buy what protection you can. When the time comes, you'll be glad you planned ahead.

You have five options:

1. Traditional long-term care insurance

2. Variable annuity with a long-term care rider

3. Lump-sum life insurance policy with a long-term care rider

4. Annual payment life insurance with a long-term care rider

5. Reverse mortgage

A few words on the options

I'll get into more detail on each potential option, but here's a quick overview first. Lower income individuals can increase their preparedness for LTC needs with an annuity with an LTC rider. These typically double the promised annual income for the time the LTC need persists. Typically, they run for the remainder of a person's life. Another viable method is to buy life insurance with an LTC rider. Costs are typically only 10 to 20 percent higher than life insurance without the rider. The reason the costs are not much greater than straight life insurance is, the insurance company pays the benefit either as a death benefit or an LTC benefit. The disadvantage to the life insurance company is that the benefit is paid sooner, not that the benefits paid are higher.

Whatever you decide, the LTC plan should be flexible and allow you to stay within your comfort zone. Policies that require institutionalization frequently fail to meet family needs and desires. Policies that exclude vital services just to lower the premiums typically leave you hanging when you need the coverage most.

Pointer: Look for policies that have a strong home health care component. Home-based long-term care services are the way of the future, and for good reason. Boomers don't want to go to a nursing home if they can "age in place."

Okay, so let's get on with Option 1.

Option 1: Traditional LTC insurance

Purchasing a traditional LTC policy is a viable option, but only if you meet certain conditions. Many retirees put off buying a traditional long-term care insurance policy until they reach age sixty, according to the US Department of Health's National Clearinghouse on Long-Term Care. That's a bad idea because the longer you wait to buy, the more expensive the insurance is going to be and the more likely something will come up that will make it impossible for you to buy long-term care insurance. Fortunately, the average age of people buying long-term care insurance offered at work is fifty, meaning they are starting to guard against the risks of exposure to the costs for long-term care when they are younger.

You will not receive underwriting for traditional long-term care insurance if any of the following apply:

- You already need long-term care services to meet two or more ADLs.
- You have AIDS or AIDS-related complex.
- You already have any form of dementia or cognitive dysfunction, including but not limited to Alzheimer's disease.
- You have multiple sclerosis, Parkinson's disease, or any other progressive neurological condition.
- You have metastatic cancer (cancer that has spread beyond its original site).
- You have any other health condition the underwriter says makes you a bad risk.

Pointer: The insurance companies only win if they don't have to pay. There's no way they'll sign up anyone who represents a distinct risk.

Costs for traditional long-term care insurance are skyrocketing due to steady increases in health care and medical services, and due to skyrocketing numbers of insured making claims on their long-term care policies. The most recent available data (2009) from the National Association of Long-Term Care Insurance (NALTC) will give you at least some idea of what you'll have to pay. Bear in mind that each policy and insurance company is different, and the premiums are based on the age when you buy the policy, the coverage you want, and the amount of benefits paid until the policy is exhausted.

The following NALTC data are for an individual who buys his or her long-term care policy at age sixty-five.

Scenario 1: The annual cost is $2,028 for a maximum daily benefit of $100 for a three-year benefit period. The individual is single and the standard "health rate" (not the preferred rate or rate with spousal discounts, etc.) applies.

Scenario 2: The annual cost is $4,867 for a maximum daily benefit of $240 for a three-year benefit period. The individual is single and the standard "health rate" (not the preferred rate or rate with spousal discounts, etc.) applies.

Recent US Department of Health and Human Services data (2011) indicates that the average daily cost of a semiprivate room in a nursing home is $198. So, the individual in Scenario 1 is partially insuring, which isn't such a bad idea if he or she has other assets that can produce income to pay the difference. It's important that income from those extra assets not be counted on for meeting other expenses. The individual in Scenario 2 is insuring for a private room and hedging against other unforeseen expenses.

Pointer: Most long-term care insurance companies offer an inflation protection component for an extra fee. Buy it!

As the data suggest, premium rates are escalating because insurance companies underestimated costs. Several major LTC insurance companies stopped selling new policies in recent years. MetLife left the market in 2010 and Prudential announced its exit from selling new business in early 2012. Major insurers are also increasing premiums. John Hancock announced in late 2010 they would ask state regulators for an average increase of 40 percent per year.

Once insurers sell LTC insurance they must receive permission from appropriate authorities within *each* state to increase premium costs. Thus, some states may grant rate increases while other states either deny increases, or grant lesser increases. Policyholders who get hit with hefty premium rate increases naturally become quite upset. Nevertheless, it is seldom right to cancel an existing LTC policy.

Existing LTC policyholders have several options when faced with premium increases. They can

- pay the higher premium and maintain the benefits they originally purchased,
- allow the benefit period to be reduced but maintain their cost-of-living increases and daily or monthly limits,
- reduce future cost-of-living increases, or
- reduce their daily benefits while maintaining both their benefit period and their cost-of-living features.

I seldom advise anyone to base *all* their future LTC protection in a traditional LTC policy. My major concern is that escalating costs may force them to abandon coverage just when they need it most. The maximum benefit coverage in these policies is typically about 50 to 80 times the annual premium. This multiple is called the leverage in LTC policies. Because the median cost of care is $73,000 per year, it is very important to cover the LTC exposure.

Option 2: Variable annuity with an LTC rider

You can use tax-deferred retirement assets, like IRAs and 401(k)s, to purchase a variable annuity with a LTC rider. The LTC rider provides for double income when a qualifying LTC need occurs after the contract has been in force for three years. This policy requires qualifying for LTC (needing help with at least two of the six activities of daily living), but it is not indemnity. Thus, if they received double benefits, they would not need to prove the level of LTC expenses.

This investment is very attractive for protecting cash flow without receiving the double income for LTC. Because this investment includes the insurance company's guarantee of future income growth, it also helps provide purchasing power and inflation protection.

Pointer: There is no underwriting requirement for this option.

Option 3: Lump-sum life insurance with an LTC rider

The third alternative is clearly my favorite for all clients who can find the initial lump sum necessary to fund it. A single lump-sum life insurance purchase will typically purchase LTC protection of 2.5 to 4.0 times the amount of the lump sum. This type of policy allows the policy owner to redeem at no cost any time prior to beginning to draw benefits. The real cost of this type of policy is the lost earnings from the policy. Advantages of this type of policy are the following:

1. The ease of qualifying for LTC protection.

2. Payment for the coverage is the loss of future earnings on the deposit. Remember, you can get your money back on request.

3. Purchase of LTC benefits with lost earnings, which are never taxed.

4. A small life insurance benefit so the policy legally qualifies as life insurance (e.g., a $100,000 lump sum may buy $130,000 of life insurance coverage for a sixty-two-year-old male).

When clients have sufficient cash reserves to purchase a life insurance policy with an LTC rider, that is preferred.

Pointer: The underwriting requirement for this option is moderate, meaning the demands that you meet specific conditions are less than they would be if you were seeking to buy traditional long-term care insurance.

Option 4: Annual payment life insurance with an LTC rider

The Pension Protection Act of 2006 allows life insurance companies to provide life insurance with LTC riders. Favorable tax rules make this a very attractive alternative. I find the cost of coverage typically is about 10 to 15 percent greater than the cost of straight life insurance. Practically, the LTC coverage simply allows benefits to be paid to the insured rather than to beneficiaries after the insured's life. Naturally, if the insured uses most of the benefits, there are less legacy assets (assets left to heirs) but the LTC exposure has been nicely covered.

Many seniors find life insurance with an LTC rider attractive because it guarantees that someone in the family will receive benefits. The portion not used to pay LTC costs of the insured is paid as a life insurance benefit to heirs.

Long-term care partnership state rules provide that partnership LTC policies provide Medicaid asset protection. For every dollar that an LTC partnership policy pays out in benefits, a dollar of assets can be protected from the long-term care Medicaid limit. Partnership policies must meet the rules for tax qualified plans under federal law.

Pointer: Strict underwriting requirements apply to this option.

Option 5: Reverse mortgage

In a sense, reverse mortgages aren't a long-term care option. They are a possible source of cash to fund one of the four options above. The dire consequences of long-term costs on you and your spouse are so great that I include a discussion on reverse mortgages here to give you another possible way you can guard against the risks. Reverse mortgages for long-term care coverage aren't for everyone, but if you have no other assets available, a reverse mortgage might be worth considering.

A reverse mortgage may meet government standards for homeowners over age sixty-two. The Internal Revenue Code even has provisions detailing tax treatments when reverse mortgages provide the means for meeting cash flow deficiencies for taxpayers age sixty-two and older. At this time, reverse mortgages are not available to younger people. A reverse mortgage provides an immediate lump sum of no more than 50 percent of a home's net investment equity or provides a monthly cash flow for the period the homeowner continues to live in the home.

When the homeowner either moves or leaves the home permanently to receive greater care in a nursing home or assisted-living facility, the mortgage is settled. There may or may not be equity or principal left for the homeowner or their heirs.

Pointer: Reverse mortgages work best for single persons with no one dependent upon them for income support. Reverse mortgages should be used only after very careful research and thought, and even then not in situations where the homeowner may not be able to remain in the home at least five years.

It's important to understand that reverse mortgages utilize the equity in your home without providing any real protection if you opt for the monthly cash flow and fail to pump it into paying for premiums on long-term care insurance or to make up for cash flow lost by making a withdrawal to buy an annuity or a lump-sum life insurance policy with a long-term care rider. Effectively, you're spending your assets. Also, the decline in real estate values over the past five years has made reverse mortgages far less attractive than they used to be. In some cases of long-held real estate, reverse mortgages can make sense, though.

Pointer: Prefer a lump-sum withdrawal of homeowner equity to purchase a lump-sum life insurance policy with an LTC rider to relying on the home to provide required assets when LTC needs arise.

Reverse mortgages do have some appeal as a means of providing for LTC needs, but as you may have gathered, I generally do not like reverse mortgages for the following reasons:

1. Fees and rates are higher than for conventional mortgages.

2. There is no leverage with reverse mortgages. Every dollar of costs is borne by the borrower. No insurance pays part of the cost.

3. Reverse mortgages are frequently explained poorly to confused seniors.

Most forms of LTC protection allow taxpayers and their heirs to retain some assets when LTC assistance is needed. These LTC partnership rules generally do not give favorable treatment to reverse mortgages.

I typically view reverse mortgages as viable only if they meet a need that cannot otherwise be met. Examples:

- purchasing long-term care insurance
- purchasing Medicare supplement coverage
- buying an annuity that promises a greater income and residual value that the reduction in net housing value
- meeting minimal monthly cash flow needs

While I seldom advise utilizing a reverse mortgage, in some cases it may be the only alternative or the best alternative. I have little sympathy for children who do not want their parents to get a reverse mortgage because it risks their inheritance. Don't fall into the legacy trap. Your kids may end up with even less if you do.

Pointer: Given increasing life expectancy for seniors, reverse mortgages should not be considered prior to age sixty-five or seventy.

As you consider your long-term care options, use the comparison table on the next page as a guide.

Table of LTC Alternatives

Feature	Traditional LTC	Annuity with LTC Rider	Lump-Sum Life Ins. with LTC Rider	Annual Payment Life Ins. with LTC Rider
Initial Payment	Annual Premium	Initial Investment	Lump-Sum Payment	Annual Premium
Premium Increase Potential	High	Little or None	Little or None	Little or None
Leverage	Typically 30+ Times Premium	Income Doubles (i.e., 5% to 10%)	Typically 2 1/2 to 4 Times Lump-Sum	Typically 30+ Times Premium
Ease of Qualification	Strict Underwriting	No Underwriting	Moderate Underwriting	Strict Underwriting
Cost If Don't Ever Need	Loss of Premiums	Slightly Lower Return	Lose Potential Earnings on Lump-Sum	Minimally Higher Premium
Cost-of-Living Coverage Increases	Available for a Cost	No, but Investment Base May Grow	Yes	Not Typically
Type of Benefits	Daily or Monthly Based upon Qualification and Reimbursement	Double-Income Monthly Based upon Qualification	Monthly Maximum for Specified Period until Benefits Are Used Up	Monthly Maximum for Specified Period until Benefits Are Used Up
Major Advantage	Lower Initial Cost and Cost-of-Living Increases	Investment Can Grow and Be Used If No LTC Need	LTC Protection Provided for Using Investor's Money Life Insurance Excess Over Initial Premium Is Small	Lower Initial Cost and No Premium Increases Life Insurance Benefit If Not Needed for LTC
Major Disadvantage	Substantial Premium Increases Are Likely	Investment Value Must Be Greater	Large Initial Deposit Required to Get Sufficient Benefits	No Cost-Living Feature

A few more words on your kids

The term "sandwich generation" was first coined in 1981 as demographers, sociologists, psychologists, and other academics began to focus on a segment of the US population between the ages of forty-five and fifty-five who began offering significant support for aging parents and dependent children. The bulk of the sandwich generation was and still is female, and the numbers are growing. As we boomers age, our kids are going to feel increasing pressure to offer us some form of care, even if it's just moral support and some happy times with the grandkids.

When things go south with us in terms of health or cognitive ability, it's most often the kids who bear the brunt of dealing with the situation. Financial drains from aging parents often seriously wound or kill a child's funds for their kids' college and weddings, and for their own retirement and that of a spouse. Don't forget your family when you're making decisions about whether to buy long-term care insurance. Believe me, the family will very likely suffer if you don't guard against the inherent risks.

That said, I'd like to present you (and your kids) with a little known tax break your kids can take advantage of if they are footing a large share of your medical bills. Sadly, many people are in this very unenviable position, and so are their parents.

Tax breaks for parental medical costs

Scenario 1

Bill is paying a lot of money to help with his mother's medical bills. Phil, Bill's accountant, and I helped carefully structure his tax situation to offset part of his mother's costs, by deducting her medical expenses on his return. Qualifying for this deduction requires the following:

- A relationship test (i.e., a qualifying child or relative).

- The taxpayer provides more than half the dependent's support (that's a very big requirement).
- The dependent earns less than the current year personal exemption amount (Social Security benefits not generally included).
- The dependent is a US citizen or resident alien.
- The dependent must live with the taxpayer (that's another big requirement, and many kids won't meet it).

Observe that Bill's mother appears to fail several dependency tests. She does not live with Bill, and her interest, dividends, and pension exceed the personal exemption amount. However, if a taxpayer cannot claim a dependent due to the gross income test, they may utilize an exception that allows them to claim medical expenses they pay for their parents.

You're not necessarily stuck if you don't meet the above criteria

If a taxpayer could claim a parent as a dependent, but the dependent's gross income exceeds the personal exemption amount, the taxpayer may still claim the parent's medical expense on their own return. The taxpayer *must* provide over half the parent's support. However, the parent need not live with the taxpayer.

I noted earlier that Phil deducted Bill's mother's medical expenses. This is a reasonable position. The problem occurred when Bill's mother's accountant argued the IRS would both deny the deduction and impose penalties on Bill's return. Bill asked me to intervene and tell him the appropriate position. Phil seldom takes a bad position. The mother's accountant forcefully took a badly informed position. Unfortunately, his misunderstanding is often a majority position for tax accountants and fails the client's best interests.

Pointer: Many (if not most) tax preparers do not know the medical expense exception that allows a taxpayer to deduct medical expenses they pay for their parents. They must pay the expense directly to an institution or care provider. They must also provide at least half the parent's support.

These expenses can be deductible but only if paid directly to care providers and/or institutions. The payor must pay at least half the total expenses of the parent. Only one child in a given tax year can claim these deduction, but the good news is, siblings can alternate claiming the dependency exemption and paying and deducting a parent's medical expenses. Caution dictates careful structuring and documenting the payments and the process. The last thing you want to do is have two or more kids claiming the same deductions in a single tax year.

Tax issues like these are very complex. Even some tax professionals don't know how to best serve their older clients or the children of older clients. If your kids are paying a significant sum to help you deal with medical and other costs, contact a tax professional specializing in issues related to aging boomers. Your kids could be eligible for some significant tax relief.

Parting words: Long-term care issues are among the hottest buttons boomers face in retirement planning and management. The notion of having to wear adult diapers or not recognizing yourself in the mirror is just simply way too traumatic for most of us to contemplate, so we just ignore these possible facets of our lives as we hit old age. The high costs of long-term care add to the tendency to "go ostrich" on this subject. As tough as it may be for you, take a good hard look at long-term care as an integral part of your retirement strategy. If you don't need the coverage, you come out a winner, especially if you don't buy a traditional long-term care insurance product. If you do plan on the worst and you end up needing assistance, at least you'll have mitigated the financial damage.

12

Hearth and Home

RETIREMENT ISN'T ALL SCARY business. In fact, once you've got all your financial ducks lined up and you know your asset limits, monthly cash flow needs, Medicare coverage (get the best you can afford), Social Security options, and long-term care counterattack if the bogeyman pays you a visit, then you're good to go. You don't have to live in fear, because you've stared reality right in the face and taken steps to protect your spouse and yourself from the dire consequences of making bad choices. That's actually a pretty cool place to be. Today, sixty-five is the new forty-five; enjoy it!

Retirement these days is a lot different from what it was for your grandparents. Older preboomers (those folks born well before 1946) didn't really view retirement as an option. The men generally worked till they dropped dead. Their wives were left alone in the house where the kids grew up, and there was no real support for them outside of friends and family. Most people of that era died before age seventy. I know it seems unbelievable, but the average life expectancy for a man in 1940 was only sixty-two! That's why the thinkers behind Social Security figured the program would work. Hardly anybody collected for more than a couple years.

Life after "the job" started to change in the early 1950s, when retirement became an option and life expectancy began to increase. Younger preboomers got the benefit of a huge economic boon time, seeing the growth of industry, the spread of suburban communities, the advent of fast food and rock 'n' roll, and the burgeoning of a love of leisure that eventually led to the explosion of the Winnebago and fiberglass powerboats in the 1960s, among many other things.

Florida became a focal point for retirees, as did much of the Sunbelt. The retiree with knee-high white tennis socks, multicolored polo shirts, and hearing aids on the golf course became a national cliché. And guess what? The preboomers didn't give a darn; they were living the good life in retirement communities made just for them. These communities arose in part because Dad got booted out the door with a gold watch in hand and had no idea of what to do next, except drive his wife nuts, and wives wanted to play just as much as their husbands. They also wanted their husbands to have something to do besides follow them around.

The active adult phenomenon

To be sure, there were "old folks homes," where men and women were sent to watch their arteries harden while ensconced in a comfy rocking chair on the porch. But a seismic change began in 1954 with the opening of a forerunner of the first modern active adult community, a development called Youngtown, built on a ranch about twenty miles outside of Phoenix, Arizona. The founder, Benjamin Schleifer, envisioned the community as a place where retirees could live on just Social Security. He saw it as a haven for older men and women with a yen to play shuffleboard, canasta, and horseshoes, and where they could have fun dancing on Saturday evenings at the clubhouse after munching down tasty potluck suppers.

The active adult concept, which is the leading type of community being built in the United States today, caught on like wildfire. Del Webb and K. Hovnanian are among the bigger homebuilders offering the active adult lifestyle, and if you think it's just a jazzed up version of Schleifer's Youngtown, think again. Sure, there are canasta games, but these communities offer a lot more than that. They restrict residents to those age fifty-five and up, offer maintenance of the grounds, and usually include a pool or two, tennis courts, pickleball courts, walking trails, an amenity center, gymnasium, clubhouse, ponds, trees, and frequently an on-site golf course. "Active adult" in gerontology circles means you're an old person who can live independently. In other words, you're an active adult. But the residents of active adult communities see themselves as active. Period. They don't even think about the technical term.

These types of communities are so popular because they offer retirees the chance to make new friends among people their own age, sharing similar interests and a commonality derived from the experience of growing gracefully older with a sense of dignity and outright fun. Ranch-style homes and the security of a gated community also draw retirees (and those fifty-five and up who are still working). The National Association of Home Builders estimated that 40 percent of all housing starts in 2012 were for a 55+ household, and it sees that market growing by as much as 25 percent in 2013.

When these communities were still developing from a conceptual point of view, many were built in the Sunbelt, based on the ongoing trends in retirement homebuilding. However, big changes began in 2001 when the first wave of boomers turned fifty-five. They've been fueling the growth of active adult communities ever since. Now, according to AARP, the majority of boomers don't want to live far from their kids and grandkids, but they do embrace the active adult lifestyle. As a consequence, developers have built active adult communities, large and small, around major metropolitan areas in the snowbelt. The market is following the desires of the boomers. Instead of going hot, it's going cold.

Aging in place

AARP studies show that 90 percent of seniors want to stay in their homes as they age, which is also known as "aging in place." When a senior requires assistance with activities of daily living or suffers from fairly major health issues, the figure drops to 82 percent. Seniors said autonomy was a leading reason why they want to stay in their own homes, with 42 percent of respondents listing living by their own rules as one of the top considerations associated with the desirability of aging in place. They also said separation from pets was a key driver for not wanting to leave home.

The ability to age in place is part of the draw of an active adult community. There is a built-in support system, though not an official one. Residents suffering from dementia or who need assistance with activities of daily living will have to bring in home-based help, or eventually move to an assisted-living or continuing-care retirement community (CCRC; more on those in a minute).

The AARP study listed some features that should be included in your home, other than being a ranch-style residence. These features include the following:

- nonslip floor surfaces, especially in bathrooms (the MetLife Mature Marketing Institute reported that 75 percent of accidental deaths among people over the age of sixty-five are from falls)
- grab bars in bathrooms
- "comfort toilets" that sit higher off the floor than conventional toilets (these are helpful for people in wheelchairs)
- wider than standard door entrances (if possible) to allow for easier wheelchair access
- entrances without steps
- lever-handled doorknobs instead of round knobs that are hard on arthritic hands
- higher electrical outlets and lower light switches (again for wheelchair users)
- security systems with personal alert functions to call emergency help

The same study cited estimates from the National Association of Homebuilders that indicates the market for remodeling existing homes to better accommodate aging boomers is between $20 and $25 billion, or about 10 percent of the current $214 billion home improvement industry. Building an aging-in-place-friendly home in an active adult community or remodeling an existing empty-nester home to make it easier for a retiree to stay well into old age is another trend on the upswing.

About assisted living

Many retirees look down their noses at assisted-living facilities as the domain of fossils in nasty high-rise warehouses. The idea of assisted living scares some people, and there are some grounds for the fears, not because the places are necessarily bad but because if you think you might need to go to one, you're having some trouble with activities of daily living. There is a tendency to deny the effects of aging. Nobody wants to think they're old and infirm, and the reality of that scenario is simply depressing. However, a time may come when you need help with some of your ADLs, but you don't need skilled nursing care. Home-based services can play a part, which is why aging in place and the growth of home health-care companies is on the rise. At some point, home-based care might not be enough to do the trick.

For example, if you find yourself all alone in the world, or with few living relatives able to lend a hand, an assisted-living environment could be the right choice for you. The sales literature often says part of the benefit is a support group of friends who are all going through the same thing you are. That's not all marketing hooey and hype. There's some truth to it. And it's not that misery loves company. People need socializing. People without it die sooner than those who have fun with their peers in the lounge or clubhouse.

The settings are often in high-rises or smaller facilities built to look like townhouse campuses or garden apartment complexes. Very few offer stand-alone homes. Dining is often communal, which some people might find a bit odious. Others might welcome the chance to interact with other people during meals. Some facilities do provide for meal preparations in your unit, but be prepared to pay for the service.

Pointer: There is no national standard in assisted-living facilities in the United States, according to AARP reports. They are licensed and regulated by each state, not the federal government.

Assisted living generally includes the following features:

- senior-friendly housing, such as a small apartment or room equipped with grab bars, nonslip floors, and so on
- some help with basic ADLs, including meal preparation, bathing, and dressing
- basic housekeeping services
- social activities

Some facilities offer limited assistance with health services, and some are associated with nursing homes in the event you need that level of service.

A few words on costs

Assisted-living facilities are in the business to make money. There are no free rides. End of story. The typical scenario is, you move in when you need a low level of service, and you find it's affordable. As soon as you need more services, you get hit with a stiff increase in the monthly bill. Read the contract very carefully before you buy into one of these facilities, and go over the contract with a lawyer or financial adviser with the expertise to guide you.

The MetLife Mature Marketing Institute pegged the average monthly cost of a typical assisted-living facility at $3,293 in 2010, up 5.2 percent from the previous year. That's a total annual cost of $39,516, a very hefty sum for most of us who don't have long-term coverage of some sort. Further, most studies show that retirees and their family foot the bill, which isn't surprising since fewer than 10 percent of seniors purchase long-term care coverage. There isn't much free help out there, just like there isn't for long-term care in nursing homes, unless you are poor enough to qualify for Medicaid. It's scary, but it's the way things are, and it's not going to get any easier for seniors as budget tightening continues in federal and state government policies.

Pointer: Build in a large margin of financial safety when planning on going into assisted living. If you don't, you could end up spending down your assets before you die. In general, if you've got a choice, you want to use your long-term care coverage only when you absolutely must have the services. Remember, your long-term care coverage will have a benefits cap.

About continuing-care retirement communities

The idea behind continuing-care retirement communities is, they offer lifetime housing for seniors and graduated levels of care all the way to dealing with dementia and major health issues. You might call them a combination of active adult community, assisted-living facility, and nursing home all in one big enchilada. The beauty of the CCRC is, you age in place, moving from the active adult section to the assisted-living section when the need becomes necessary, and from there your last stop is the nursing home unit. It sounds a bit ghoulish to some, I know. But on the other hand, the concept does have merit. After all, you might not need assisted living or long-term skilled nursing, so you don't have to pay for those services until you do need them, if you go for a fee-for-service contract (more on that later). Of course, you don't have to pay for those levels of service if you don't need them in a pure active adult setting or in a traditional empty-nester home.

Pointer: Seniors often pay for more expensive plans that cover assisted living and skilled nursing just to be sure they can receive those services, if necessary, and to build the cash outflow into their financial planning.

CCRCs have been around for decades, and they cater to the more affluent. The settings are typically in an upscale campus composed of different kinds of units (usually multidwelling), ranging from single studio apartments to quasi-townhouse residences for residents who are "active adults," meaning they can live independently without assistance with ADLs. There are also assisted-living quarters and fully staffed nursing home facilities. Swimming pools, tennis courts, health clubs, club houses, and other amenities are often found in the better CCRCs. Again, the idea is to cater to your needs from early old age to extended old age. Nearly one million Americans were living in CCRCs in 2010, says data from the American Association of Homes and Services for the Aging. The number is expected to increase dramatically in the future, as boomers hit age seventy and up, which is going to happen in 2016 when the first wave of boomers reaches their seventh decade of life.

As is the case with assisted-living facilities, the federal government doesn't regulate or license CCRCs. That's up to the state, which means you will find various levels of legal protection, diverse standards of living and care, and wide differences in allowable rates.

Pointer: The key value of a CCRC is that you don't get booted when things get tough, whereas you'll have to move at least twice (traditional home to active adult and on to assisted living) outside of a CCRC setting. You may have to move a third time if you require skilled nursing care. Picking up and going because things have gotten bad is emotionally trying for you and your loved ones.

A few words on costs

Sit tight; your jaw might drop!

As previously noted, CCRCs typically cater to the wealthier among us.

Here's how it works. You put down a hefty deposit, regardless of which level of care you need. At the time of the buy-in, you choose a contract that will provide the menu of services you want or need. You pay a monthly fee for those contracted services. So far, so good.

According to the National Investment Center for Seniors Housing and Care Industry, a Maryland-based industry trade group involved in CCRCs, in 2010 the average CCRC entrance fee nationwide was $249,857. However, the buy-in can change depending on the level of contract you want (see below). The buy-in fee isn't necessarily refundable if you die or move out, but some contracts allow for refunds under very specific circumstances. All fees listed below come from 2010 data from the US Government Accountability Office (GAO), the most recent data available.

There are several contract levels:

- life care
- modified
- fee-for-service
- rental

Life care: Consider this one a Rolls-Royce agreement. Essentially, you pay a whopping monthly fee no matter what level of care you need, but you're fully covered for whatever might crop up down the road. The fee covers housing, meals, and amenities.

Entry fee: $160,000 to $600,000

Monthly cost: $2,500 to $5,400

Modified: Consider this one a Lexus agreement. You get a nice ride at a lower cost, but you also get fewer services. As soon as you need more services than you thought when you signed up, your fees go up. What you're doing with this contract level is betting you'll stay as healthy as you were when you showed up at the door.

Entry fee: $80,000 to $750,000

Monthly cost: $1,500 to $2,500

The above monthly fees apply for independent living, assisted living, and skilled nursing home living. The fees don't change when you trade up for a higher level of service. Monthly fees go up for independent living, assisted living, and skilled nursing home living for fee-for-service and rental contract levels (see below).

Fee-for-service: Consider this one a Honda Accord agreement. Your monthly fees only cover housing, meals, and amenities. You pay for all your required health- and living-related services. If you want to move up to a new contract level, you pay. Some CCRCs lock you into your contract or charge you hefty fees to modify the contract you sign when you move in.

Entry fee: $100,000 to $500,000

Monthly cost, independent living: $1,300 to $4,300

Monthly cost, assisted living: $3,700 to $5,800

Monthly cost, nursing home living: $8,100 to $10,000

Rental: Consider this one a Rent-a-Wreck agreement. You're getting the bare minimum. It's essentially pay-as-you-go, and you pay big for not signing up for a Rolls or a Lexus if you need enhanced services beyond independent living. While the US Government Accountability Office data gives a price range for the rental entry fee, in most cases, CCRCs waive the entry fee. The owners of these businesses know they'll probably get you to pay more at a later time.

Entry fee: $1,800 to $30,000

Monthly cost, independent living: $900 to $2,700

Monthly cost, assisted living: $4,700 to $6,500

Monthly cost, nursing home living: $8,100 to $10,700

The above fees from GAO 2010 data should be highly revealing about how CCRCs work—highlighting how these businesses leverage services against contract levels and fees. There's nothing nefarious about CCRCs. For some people, they're great! But the GAO report warns consumers that extreme caution should be exercised when considering a CCRC; they should be considered an investment, as opposed to simply a place to live. If a CCRC goes under or gets into financial trouble, you might lose your entrance fee (even if your contract says it's refundable), and you might find services that were once free now incur a fee. Staff layoffs, deferred opening of assisted-living or nursing care facilities, and any number of other risks occur if your CCRC hits the skids. Of course, assisted-living facilities may also encounter financial trouble, and active adult communities that are poorly run will give you less service for higher homeowner association fees.

There's no perfect world in retirement living. But there are some great options out there for you to look at. Just do your homework and seek guidance from experts. Always look before you leap!

Parting words: As you can see from these pages, retirement issues cover a broad spectrum. You can't just focus on investments, which is a common mistake many would-be and current retirees make. You need to look at the big picture, viewing the various components as pieces of a grand puzzle. Your goal is to assess what you have to work with, and then fit all the pieces of that puzzle together to create the gorgeous picture that will be yours to keep as your retirement years tick by. That picture could be of swaying palm trees on a Caribbean island, the rolling green of a golf course, the deck of a cruise ship, a comfortable home in an active adult community, or anything you can afford to imagine. Your retirement is as unique as you are, but as boomers, we all share much in common when it comes to the issues—finances, Social Security, Medicare, long-term care, and where we choose to live. With the right choices, you can make your resources work for you!

It's time to grab that golden ring! It's time to enjoy your time in the sun! This is your time to live the life you've worked for!

Index

lifetime reserve for hospital stays, under
    Medicare Part A, 97–98
liquidity
    balancing cash flow needs for, 127
    vs. cash flow, 16, 56
    restricting illiquid investments,
        126
    in traded REITs market, 63
living benefits, variable annuities with,
    57–58, 60–61, 63–64, 124
Long-Term Care (LTC)
    annual payment life insurance with
        LTC rider for paying, 149–50,
        153
    as assistance in activities of daily
        living, 140–41
    comparison of payment alternatives
        for, 153
    cost of, 143
    costs of, 140
    lump-sum life insurance with an
        LTC rider for paying, 149, 153
    Medicare and, 141–42
    needs and aging, 21
    in nursing homes, 140
    options in paying for, 144–52
    partnership, 150, 152
    planning, 7, 15, 20
    provided by children, 154
    provided by family and friends,
        139
    question to tax adviser on, 31
    reverse mortgages for paying,
        150–53
    risks associated with, 142–44
    tax breaks for parental medical
        costs, 154–56
    traditional LTC insurance policies
        for paying, 145–48, 153
    variable annuities LTC rider for
        paying, 148, 153

whole-life insurance rider for, 138
losses/income, IRS categories of, 37
low income retirees, Medicare and, 100–
    101, 120
lump sum
    life insurance with an LTC rider,
        149, 153
    withdrawal on pensions, 124

M

MAGI (Modified Adjusted Gross
    Income), taxing Social Security
    benefits using, 82
Major Medical, 98
markets. see stocks
Master Limited Partnerships (MLPs),
    Energy, 65
Medicaid
    asset protection with partnership
        LTC policies, 150
    long-term care and, 8
    Medicare Advantage plans and,
        116
    Supplemental Security Income and,
        73–74
medical care. see health care
medical services
    under Medicare Part B, 99
    Medicare supplement plans for,
        106–7
Medicare
    about, 95–96
    appeals due to changed
        circumstances, 99
    comparison table of plans, 118–19
    contributions to, 69
    eligibility period for, 107, 117, 118
    long-term care and, 141–42
    Part A, 97–98, 100–101, 105–7
    Part B, 98–99, 106–7, 112

insurance specialists, 31
tax professionals, 30–31, 35–39
Prudential, long-term care insurance at, 147
Public Storage, 64
purchasing power, inflation and, 20, 21–22

Q

qualifying earnings for Social Security, 69–70
qualifying hospital stay, under Medicare Part A, 97
Quinn, Jane Bryant, on variable annuities with living benefits, 63–64

R

Real Estate Investment Trusts (REITs)
  as alternative investment, xii, 55–56, 61–64
  delay drawing on nontraded, 124
  equity loans vs. nontraded public, 16
renal failure, end-stage, Medicare and, 97
rental contract, CCRC, 166
repaying Social Security benefits, to change plans, 91
retirement
  about, 1, 27
  asset allocation, 132–33
  baby boomers reaching age of, 1–2
  cash flow as foundation of, xii
  instruments having protection against inflation, 133
  measuring readiness for, 20–22
  mistakes in planning, 3–10
  preboomers and, 157–58
  taking responsibility for, xiii
  timing, 12

retirement benefits, Social Security. *see* Social Security
retirement expenses vs. cash flow, 17–18
retirement income, from part-time work, 13–14
retirement pensions
  converting to expected economic value over life expectancy, 127
  final pay in, 71
  vs. lump sums withdrawal, 124
  replacement for, 57
retirement preparation, asset accumulation and, 2
retirement readiness evaluation tool, online, 25
retirement strategies
  about, 121–22
  distributing Roth IRAs, 129
  drawing cash first, 127–28
  drawing down on assets, 126–27, 138
  life insurance in, 134–38
  lump sums withdrawal on pensions, 124
  maximizing tax deferrals, 124–26
  reducing income taxes, 122–23
  retirement asset allocation, 132–33
  timing of retirement, 129–32
reverse mortgages, 10, 150–53
risk
  associated with long-term care, 142–44
  cash flow needs and, 49
  sequence, 129–32
risk assumption decisions, 110–11
ROKA Wealth Strategists, vii
Roosevelt, Franklin D., 67
Roth IRA accounts, 38–39, 51–53, 129
Rubin, Robert, 65
rules
  for evaluating investments, 61–62

for Medicare Advantage plans, 114

CPSIA information can be obtained at www.ICGtesting.com
Printed in the USA
LVOW13s2249120813

347534LV00002B/4/P